ADVENTURE INTO SILENCE

ADVENTURE INTO SILENCE

Making a Private Retreat

Augustine Hoey Ob. OSB

DARTON·LONGMAN + TODD

First published in 2000 by
Darton, Longman and Todd Ltd
1 Spencer Court
140–142 Wandsworth High Street
London SW18 4JJ

ISBN 0–232–52343–6

A catalogue record for this book is available from the British Library.

Designed by Sandie Boccacci
Phototypeset in 11/14pt Aldus
by Intype London Ltd
Printed and bound in Great Britain
by Redwood Books, Trowbridge, Wiltshire.

In memory of my sister Patricia

Contents

Preface

If we take a pencil and underline all those passages in the gospels which describe Our Lord at prayer we find that he often went apart in order to find silence and pray by himself. 'After sending the crowds away he went up into the hills by himself to pray' (Matt. 14:23). 'Then Jesus came with them to a small estate called Gethsemane; and he said to his disciples, "Stay here while I go over there to pray"' (Matt. 26:36). 'In the morning, long before dawn, he got up and left the house, and went off to a lonely place and prayed there' (Mark 1:35). 'After saying goodbye to them he went off into the hills to pray' (Mark 6:46). 'They came to a small estate called Gethsemane, and Jesus said to his disciples, "Stay here while I pray". Then he took Peter and James and John with him. And a sudden fear came over him, and great distress. And he said to them, "Wait here and keep awake." AND GOING ON A LITTLE FURTHER HE THREW HIMSELF ON THE GROUND AND PRAYED . . .' (Mark 14:32–35). 'His reputation continued to grow, and large crowds would gather to hear him and to have their sickness cured, BUT HE WOULD ALWAYS GO OFF TO SOME PLACE WHERE HE COULD BE ALONE AND PRAY' (Luke 5:16). 'Now it was about this time that he went out into the hills to pray; and he spent the whole night in prayer to God' (Luke 6:12). 'Now one day when he was praying alone . . .' (Luke 9:18). 'Now about eight days after this had been said, he took with him Peter and John and James and went up the mountain to pray' (Luke 9:28). 'Then he withdrew from them, about a stone's throw away, and knelt down and prayed' (Luke 22:41).

So, it would seem that much of the prayer life of Our Lord was spent alone and often with a deliberate separation from his disciples and other familiar faces. We, who in our Christian endeavour are struggling to 'put on Christ' must try to do the same. In modern terms this is called making a retreat. A retreat is not confined to 'specially religious people', but is meant for us all. I pray that what is written in the following pages will help you to make a retreat.

Augustine Hoey ob. OSB
Autumn 1999

Introduction

Many people, laity, priests and the religious, make a private retreat. They go away to a retreat house, a monastery, a convent, or, if it is practical, they stay on home ground, to be alone with God. It is a brief journey into the wilderness with Our Lord. The wilderness is a place of silence. Silence is the sound of God and is a MUST for a retreat. Silence is the most important aspect of a retreat. It gives God an opportunity to speak to us as we sit in silence before him. Meals should be taken in silence. Talking is not the only way of breaking silence. Other ways include:

1) the TV, the radio, the telephone and the newspapers;
2) reading too many books and thereby stuffing our minds with other people's ideas about God and leaving no space for God to speak to us. Ideally the Bible is the only reading we should allow ourselves when in retreat;
3) writing letters and making up our late correspondence;
4) making it a time for preparing homilies, writing articles, etc.

There are two kinds of wilderness

1) The one described by Our Lord. He and the disciples had been ministering all day to the needs of the sick and afflicted. The pressures were enormous and unending. There was no time even to eat. Finally, Our Lord said to

the disciples, 'You must come away to some lonely place [the wilderness] all by yourselves and rest for a while' (Mark 6:31).

We may need a retreat for the same reason; feeling stressed we want to withdraw and rest awhile. Sleep is an important part of a retreat and we should not feel guilty if we find ourselves 'dozing off'. The Holy Spirit never sleeps and is often very active within us when we are asleep. Think of the messages St Joseph received while he was asleep:

(i) the decision to go ahead and marry Mary even though he was baffled by her pregnancy (Matt. 1:18–25);

(ii) the decision to flee with Mary and the child into Egypt to escape the murderous wrath of Herod (Matt. 2:13–15);

(iii) the decision as to when was the right moment to return home to the land of Israel and where to settle (Matt. 2:19–23).

2) The wilderness of temptation (Matt. 4:1–11). After his baptism Our Lord withdrew to the wilderness to prepare for his public ministry. He was violently tempted to take short cuts about it. The struggle was intense. So, too, in retreat we may find little peace of mind or rest. We feel beset on all sides by distraction, anxiety, restlessness, boredom, and a feeling that God is absent. This may be because we have rightly gone into retreat with a problem. It may have something to do with marriage, family life, a situation at work, or whether we have a vocation to the priesthood or to a monastery or convent. A decision has to be made and the struggle is part of it. St Matthew tells us that after Our Lord had made his decisions 'angels appeared and looked after him'. So, too, after we have made a right decision, there is a sense of relief and inner

tranquillity; this will persist through all the difficulties of acting on the decision.

Part of a retreat should be spent sitting and DOING NOTHING. This is not an easy exercise because we normally live such hectic and pressured lives in a society addicted to activism. To sit and do nothing overwhelms us with a sense of guilt and restlessness. In the poetic account of God creating the world (Gen. 1:1—2:3) we are told that on the seventh day God rested all day. He did nothing. What are we meant to learn from this? To sit in silence and do nothing is a wonderful relaxation and a time of awareness of God around us and within us. 'Be still and know that I am God' (Ps. 46:10).

If at the end of the retreat you feel 'flat', disappointed because you feel you have got nothing out of it, everything feels just the same as before, don't worry. God has scattered his seeds. It will take time for them to grow and mature. A retreat always has a profound effect on us and time will make this clear.

On arrival at the place of retreat find out the times of meals and then plan a timetable for yourself. It should include:

1) Daily Eucharist.
2) If the place of retreat is monastic or some other place where offices are said regularly, DON'T THINK YOU MUST ATTEND THEM. Make your own decision about this. Go to some, one or none.
3) Spend an hour on each of the following meditations. One in the morning and the other in the afternoon or evening.
4) A time for relaxation, resting or taking a walk.
5) Thirty minutes sitting, DOING NOTHING (preferably before the Blessed Sacrament).

6) Time of rising in the morning and putting out the light at night.

Here are four two-day retreats for lay people, readers, catechists, Eucharistic Ministers, etc.:

  I. On the resurrection.
 II. On the triumph of the cross and passion.
III. Going into retreat with Mary, mother of the Lord.
IV. A patchwork retreat.

CHOOSE ONE and, having chosen, stick with it. Don't go leafing among others.

I. A Retreat on the Resurrection

Before beginning a meditation sit still for a few minutes, saying slowly several times, 'Holy Spirit of God dwelling within me, teach me and enlighten me during this time of meditation.'

FIRST MEDITATION

John 20:1–2, 11–18.

v.1 It was very early on the first day of the week and still dark, when Mary of Magdala came to the tomb. She saw that the stone had been moved away from the tomb and came running to Simon Peter and the other disciple, the one Jesus loved. 'They have taken the Lord out of the tomb' she said 'and we don't know where they have put him.'

v.11 Meanwhile Mary stayed outside near the tomb, weeping.

v.12 Then, still weeping, she stooped to look inside, and saw two angels in white sitting where the body of Jesus had been, one at the head, the other at the feet.

v.13 They said, 'Woman, why are you weeping?' 'They have taken my Lord away' she replied 'and I don't know where they have put him.'

v.14 As she said this she turned round and saw Jesus standing there, though she did not recognise him.

v.15 Jesus said, 'Woman, why are you weeping? Who are you looking for?' Supposing him to be the gardener, she said, 'Sir, if you have taken him away, tell me where you have put him, and I will go and remove him'.

v.16 Jesus said, 'Mary!' She knew him then and said to him in Hebrew, 'Rabbuni!' – which means Master.

v.17   Jesus said to her, 'Do not cling to me, because I have not yet ascended to the Father. But go and find the brothers and tell them: I am ascending to my Father and your Father, to my God and your God.'

v.18   So Mary of Magdala went and told the disciples that she had seen the Lord and that he had said these things to her.

Reflection

vv.1–2   These verses suggest panic on Mary of Magdala's part ... panic when the totally unexpected happens about some situation or someone who concerns us very deeply. The old securities have gone ... for Mary of Magdala the death and burial of Our Lord were a finale. It could not be worse, the former stimulating and all-embracing relationship with him was finished. Yet, she could hang on to the memory of it and live it all over again at the grave. But the one link necessary to this – the body – had disappeared. She felt the foundations of her life were crumbling to pieces.

We often feel like that when some unexpected disaster cuts across our lives and jettisons the whole of our past. It may be that my husband or wife is wanting to divorce me; my son or daughter is on drugs; I have been made redundant; someone I trusted has let me down; someone I love has developed AIDS. Or perhaps God may present us with a vocation to the priesthood, to the monastery or the convent, when we would prefer to keep to our accustomed work and lifestyle. It feels, as the Psalmist says, as if 'all thy waves and storms are gone over me'. The same experience overwhelms us when someone very near and dear to us dies suddenly and for the moment we feel there is nothing left worth living for.

v.11 There is a great emphasis on her weeping. Was her grief so self-centred and absorbing, was she so broken that the past was over and the future seemed to hold nothing, that she had become the victim of her own emotion? Grief can become like this in any bereavement. There is always a legitimate place for tears and it always takes time to adjust, sometimes quite a long time, to the new situation. But for some it can turn sour and become a self-absorption and an excuse for getting out of things, a withdrawal and a demand for constant special consideration. Thus it becomes a form of self-pity, but it parades as a virtue; a devotion to the memory of someone. Queen Victoria was like this about the unexpected death of her husband, Albert, the Prince Consort. Mary of Magdala had become so obsessed by her grief that all reason had flown out of the window and she had become unteachable.

vv.12–13 Even conversation with two angels could not rouse her from her emotional self-pity. Like her, so often we cannot see the truth because we have blind spots. We just don't listen. We don't want to. We just cannot see the truth in a situation. We are unteachable. We have got twisted around ourselves and cannot bear to let go of the old securities, the old ideas or even admit we are mistaken. We are blind to the obvious.

v.14 So she did not even recognise Jesus.

v.15 She makes wild, extravagant and impossible statements. How could she possibly have coped with carrying a corpse alone? Acceptance of disturbing and bewildering situations in our marriage, in family life, at our work place, in the Church or in illness and disability is probably not our strong point. We often make things very difficult for ourselves and for others because we will not accept new situations. Yes, we will accept sacrificial feats, 'carrying the corpse alone', so long as we can have things as we want them to be, without ever considering that our wants may be completely unreal and out of touch with the contemporary situation.

v.16 The familiar sound of his voice is needed to rouse her from her self-centred, all-absorbing mourning and the incident brings vividly before us Our Lord's own words on the good shepherd ' . . . the sheep hear his voice, one by one he calls his own sheep and leads them out . . . the sheep follow because they know his voice. They never follow a stranger but run away from him: they do not recognise the voice of strangers' (John 10:3–5). Our Lord calls us 'one by one'. Every single man, woman and child is an individual creation. Our names are so important to God. The truth of the resurrection was revealed to Mary of Magdala by the sound of her name. She recognised the sound of the voice as she had so often heard it in the past. Elsewhere in the Bible, Simon became Peter. Saul became Paul. Zechariah is told by the angel that the son his wife is to bear him is to be called John. There was something very special about this, bringing forth a protest from the family that they had never had anyone called that before (Luke 1:11–13, 57–66). When God sent the archangel Gabriel to ask Mary if she would be willing to become the mother of his Son he said 'you must name him Jesus' (Luke 1:31).

v.17 It is obvious from Our Lord's words, 'Do not cling to me', that, as one might have expected with Mary of Magdala, she had flung herself at him. Perhaps she was thinking that now he was there, everything would be as it had always been. Her gesture was the symbol of her desire to keep him to herself, to recapture and try to hang on to the past. But Our Lord deliberately points her away from it into the future.

There is never any going back. Yet, how often we waste time fretting and fuming and sighing to recapture the past – a past which, in any case, we glamorise, because it never was as we like to think it was. We are to mature and move on into ever deeper relationships with God and with each other, and the possible darkness and bewilderment of the moment are part of this deepening. We have here no abiding city. We are on a pilgrimage and leaving things behind; we are to press on to those which are ahead.

Our Lord is telling Mary of Magdala that their future relationship is to have a completely new dimension when he says, 'I am ascending to my Father and your Father, to my God and your God.' Why does Our Lord say ' . . . my Father and your Father . . .'? Why not 'Our Father'? It emphasises who he really is, that although he is man he is God. Yes, the disciples, like Mary of Magdala, are sons and daughters with him of the same Father. They by adoption (like us at our baptism), he by essence (so in the creed we say of Our Lord 'being of one substance with the Father'). We in him through baptism, he in himself. Our Father is his father, Our God is his God, yet in different relationships. The risen Lord directs our thoughts at once, not to his resurrection, but to the fact that it is the means of attaining our real home with him in heaven. 'He only could unlock the door of heaven and let us in.' 'I am ascending', he said to Mary of Magdala. She is to keep looking up and beyond. The Lord's prayer directs us to do the same in its opening words, 'Our Father, who art in heaven . . .'

Yes, if that dead body had been there, Mary of Magdala

would have had a great devotion to it. She would have visited the tomb regularly, taking fresh flowers, indulging the cult of memory, for which people would have respected her. We, too, have to take great care not to reduce the Christian faith to the self-sacrificing cult of memory, hugging it to ourselves as our own personal and private possession.

v.18   Mary of Magdala was bidden not to linger, ' . . . go and find the brothers and tell them'. So she did, although perhaps she would have preferred to stay with Our Lord in the garden. It makes us reflect on how good are we at telling others about the wonder of the Christian faith and how it alone can give meaning and purpose to life and all because Christ is risen? It is impossible to be a Christian if we lack the urge to tell others the good news. 'My beloved is happy and this fills me with a profound happiness that I have to spread' (Charles de Foucauld).

Turn back and read the gospel passage from John chapter 20 twice, slowly, reflectively. What is it saying to you?

vv.1–2   The panic of Mary Magdalene. What are the things that cause me to panic? What are the things I'm hanging onto in life? Some person? Or a way of doing things? How will I cope when they are removed?

v.12   Emphasis on 'weeping'; self-centred, absorbing grief – obsessional. Have I got obsessions? What are they? Why are they?

vv.13–14   Do I refuse to listen to what others are saying? How do I accept disturbing situations – political; at work; in the family; in the Church; in relationships?

v.16   Jesus called Mary Magdalene by her name. Her own

individuality was summed up and recognised in her name. What does your name mean to you?

v.17 'cling' – Mary in her extravagant gesture thought that she had got the whole of the past back and everything was going to be marvellous again. Do I think like this? Can the past be recalled? Should not relationships always be taking on new dimensions? Reflect on your own relationships. The resurrection is not a return to the familiar; the risen Christ is the same and yet different (not always immediately recognisable).

The whole episode brings home the bewildering truth that Jesus, dead or alive, is never where we expect him to be. Mary fully expected him to be in the tomb and not in the guise of a gardener! Do I only look for him in a religious setting?

When I have a sense of loss of God do I spend my time weeping like Mary did instead of realising that the empty silence is a new and different experience of God?

Sit for 15 minutes DOING NOTHING.

SECOND MEDITATION

Luke 24:13–25 (The road to Emmaus).

v.13   That very same day, two of them were on their way to a village called Emmaus, seven miles from Jerusalem,

v.14   and they were talking together about all that had happened.

v.15   Now as they talked this over, Jesus himself came up and walked by their side;

v.16   but something prevented them from recognising him.

v.16   He said to them, 'What matters are you discussing as you walk along?'

v.17   They stopped short, their faces downcast.

v.18   Then one of them, called Cleopas, answered him, 'You must be the only person staying in Jerusalem who does not know the things that have been happening there these last few days.'

v.19   'What things?' he asked. 'All about Jesus of Nazareth' they answered 'who proved he was a great prophet by the things he said and did in the sight of God and of the whole people;

v.20   and how our chief priests and our leaders handed him over to be sentenced to death, and had him crucified.

v.21   Our own hope had been that he would be the one to set Israel free.

v.22 And this is not all: two whole days have gone by since it all happened; and some women from our group have astounded us: they went to the tomb in the early morning,

v.23 and when they did not find the body, they came back to tell us they had seen a vision of angels who declared he was alive.

v.24 Some of our friends went to the tomb and found everything exactly as the women had reported, but of him they saw nothing.'

v.25 Then he said to them, 'You foolish men! So slow to believe the full message of the prophets!

v.26 Was it not ordained that the Christ should suffer and so enter into his glory?'

v.27 Then, starting with Moses and going through all the prophets, he explained to them the passages throughout the scriptures that were about himself.

v.28 When they drew near to the village to which they were going, he made as if to go on; but they pressed him to stay with them.

v.29 'It is nearly evening' they said 'and the day is almost over.' So he went in to stay with them.

v.30 Now while he was with them at table, he took the bread and said the blessing; then he broke it and handed it to them.

v.31 And their eyes were opened and they recognised him; but he had vanished from their sight.

v.32 Then they said to each other, 'Did not our hearts burn within us as he talked to us on the road and explained the scriptures to us?'

v.33 They set out that instant and returned to Jerusalem.

There they found the Eleven assembled together with their companions,

v.34   who said to them, 'Yes, it is true. The Lord has risen and has appeared to Simon.'

v.35   Then they told their story of what had happened on the road and how they had recognised him at the breaking of bread.

Reflection

Such resurrection appearances as we have knowledge of fulfilled the aspirations of very different individuals. Mary Magdalene is the emotional type who has intense relationships. She thinks with her heart. The two men on the road to Emmaus are more the rational type, who think with their minds. 'Our own hope had been that he would be the one to set Israel free' (v.21). Perhaps their hopes had political implications. They wanted to be free from the yoke of the Roman Empire.

v.16   There is something mysterious here. How odd that they should not recognise him, especially as their minds were full of him and they were talking about him! It is so easy to get involved in religious controversy, reading too many religious books and periodicals, arguing about Christ and the Church, etc., so that in the end we quite lose sight of the real purpose of it all which is to help us live the Christian life more authentically. Our ecclesiastical argument can blind us to the real Christ. He longs to take us over, to rise within us, and through us to reveal the power of the resurrection to all the world. Our theological debate can sometimes prevent it happening. So it defeats its own ends.

vv.18–19   They want to believe. They had great hopes in Christ, in his concern for all individuals, his care of the sick, his vision of new relationships of openness and forgiveness. They had hoped he would be successful in all the normal sense of that word. That it should all end in apparent failure was more than they could either bear or understand.

v.20   The cross was their stumbling block. It so often is, isn't it? It lies beneath our questioning as we view on our television screens the anguish and utter misery of so many and we expostulate, 'How can God love?' Yet suffering is the only way into the heart of God. The cross makes this clear. God is never absent from suffering. He is always in the midst of it. We see it in the helplessness of Christ on the cross, and in his desolation, rejection, betrayal, desertion, mockery, scourging and final dying. We must not be blind to the fact that the passion of Christ is always with us, in some shape or form. Listening to the news on radio or television is so often like following the Stations of the Cross. There is no short cut around the hill of Calvary. The resurrection lies on the other side of it and there is no other path except over it.

vv.21–24   A foreshadowing of all the debate which has occupied Christendom ever since. It has even led to wars, bigotry, fanaticism, persecution, hatred and division. This has undermined the faith of so many. The situation has not gone away. Everything depends on the answer to the question, 'Who is Christ? Man or God? Sane or mad?' Was the tomb really empty? Is the resurrection of Christ purely a spiritual matter, or did he rise body and soul?

The resurrection of Christ is an extravagant, exciting and

joyful claim. It is unique. But is it very evident in the lives of Christians? Are we too much like the two men on the Emmaus road who 'stopped short, their faces downcast' (v.17)? Christians should be radiant with expectancy. If we believe in the resurrection it gives a whole new meaning to life, and death is a gateway to total fulfilment. Yet we go on weeping and wailing, complaining and grumbling, wringing our hands and giving the truth to the philosopher, Nietzsche, who said, 'Christians must look much more saved if they want me to believe them!' We should be known the world over as 'the forgiving people' with a reputation for reconciliation. Why is it that we don't stand out more from the general run of people? Instead, we give way to the same fears, the same cults of materialism, money and sex. The same impetus for status symbols, the same compromise and hopelessness about the future. We dither and argue like the two men on the road to Emmaus. Do we still earn the rebuke of the risen Lord to those two men, 'You foolish men! So slow to believe . . .' We should question ourselves. In what way should our perspectives differ from the general outlook on the world, because we believe Christ is risen?

v.27 Our Lord's exegesis of the Old Testament. Do we find the Old Testament a confusing and baffling collection of books, shocking and contradictory and running with blood-shed? Or do we find everywhere in it the gradual unfolding of the Christ who is to come? Can we say what those two men said when we listen to the Old Testament readings at Mass, 'Did not our hearts burn within us as he talked to us on the road and explained the scriptures to us?' The 'life through death' theme runs like a golden thread through the Old Testament, preparing the way for Easter:

- Noah lived through the seeming death of the flood (Gen. 7; 8).
- Joseph 'died and rose' in Egypt (Gen. 39:7—41:45).
- Moses brought the Israelites through the death of the Red Sea to new life (Exod. 14).
- Isaac ready for death, lives (Gen. 22).
- The Jews rise from the death of exile in Babylon to return to new life in Jerusalem (Isa. 60:1–6).

vv.28–29 Our Lord never forces himself upon us. He does everything for us and then waits for our invitation. 'They pressed him to stay with them . . . so he went in to stay with them.' Then when we have let him take over, everything falls into place. But there has to be that initial choosing. Is there any particular choice he is asking of you at the moment? Then make it and you will find, as the two men did, that everything falls into place.

vv.30–31 'When he was at the table, he took the bread and said the blessing; then he broke it and handed it to them. And their eyes were opened and they recognised him, but he had vanished from their sight.' 'Vanished'. This can be our experience too. Just when we have found him and are settling down, he disappears. We are called to further searching. Our life on this earth is a pilgrimage. We are always on the move and our relationship with Our Lord is constantly changing, deepening and maturing.

He was known to the two men in the breaking of the bread. He had said, 'I am the bread of life' (John 6:35). The Eucharist, the blessed sacrament, brings the risen Christ into our midst. Jesus said, 'And know that I am with you always; yes, to the end of time' (Matt. 28:20). So he is at the altar and in the reserved sacrament. He dwells in our midst in the blessed sacrament in total silence. ('How silently, how silently, the wondrous gift is given.') The blessed sacrament is the pledge of eternal life. ' . . . anyone who eats this bread will live for ever' (John 6:58). Sunday by Sunday, and perhaps daily, we greet the risen Lord in the breaking of bread. 'Give us this day our daily bread.'

v.33   They went off immediately to tell the others. It was the middle of the night, when no one travelled for fear of brigands. The impact of the risen Christ always fills us urgently to pass on the good news. So again we are confronted by the question of how do we pass on this good news in our day and age? Do we keep it to ourselves? If so, why?

vv.34–35   Why did Our Lord make a special appearance of himself to Peter? It was because he knew how burdened Peter was by his denial and desertion of him at a very crucial moment (Luke 22:54–62). So in this lone appearance to Peter he gave him the opportunity to make his confession and be reconciled once again.

Read very slowly and with pauses Luke 24:13–35. Spend 30 minutes on this.

Is this story of a journey in any way a reflection of the journey of my own life? In what way?

v.15   They didn't recognise him! Am I so wrapped up in religious discussion, religious books and Church affairs that I have lost sight of Jesus and who he is? Write down on a sheet of paper a list of all the places (and people) where you meet Jesus other than in a religious context.

v.21   Jesus had not come up to their expectations. Has he come up to mine? Has the Church? Whose fault is it?

v.17   ' . . . faces downcast'. Am I a downcast and sad

Christian? Am I full of hope as I live in the midst of a secular, materialistic and violent society? In what ways do I bear witness to Christ in my own home, my work and my recreational situations?

v.27 Our Lord never forces himself upon us. He waits for an invitation ' . . . they pressed him to stay with them . . .' Are there some places and situations in my own life that I don't want to invite him into?

v.32 Just when they thought they had got him to themselves he disappeared! It seems as if in our Christian pilgrimage through life God plays hide and seek with us. We loved playing hide and seek when we were children; it was full of exhilaration, excitement, expectancy and appreciation. Do I find it the same with God?

v.35 They passed on the good news of their experience of the resurrection. How do I do this?

In what ways does my commitment to Christ make me stand out as being different from the general run of men and women in good natured (on the whole!), pagan, secularised England?

Sit for 15 minutes DOING NOTHING.

THIRD MEDITATION

John 20:19–23 (The risen Christ appears to his disciples).

v.19 In the evening of that same day, the first day of the week, the doors were closed in the room where the disciples were, for fear of the Jews. Jesus came and stood among them. He said to them, 'Peace be with you',

v.20 and showed them his hands and his side. The disciples were filled with joy when they saw the Lord,

v.21 and he said to them again, 'Peace be with you. As the Father sent me, so am I sending you.'

v.22 After saying this he breathed on them and said: 'Receive the Holy Spirit.

v.23 For those whose sins you forgive, they are forgiven; for those whose sins you retain, they are retained.'

Reflection

v.19 ' . . . the first day of the week'. A Sunday. All the generations of meaning which have marked out this day for Christians as different, as a day for worship and gratitude for the resurrection, are fast disappearing in our secular society. Sunday has been reduced to just another working day. This is a threat to family life. How can we best bring up our children to observe Sunday as different and special, a day to which they look forward and for which they are prepared to be mocked by their friends?

' . . . the doors were closed . . . for fear of the Jews'. A homely touch of fear and anxiety. There had been so many rumours during the day. Certainly the tomb was empty. They were frightened of being accused of having deliberately hidden the body somewhere, so they could continue to arouse interest in and promulgate the revolutionary teaching of Christ. We don't shut the doors now when we meet. But we do often live a kind of shut-in ghetto existence, only concerned with our fellow Christians. And when we are mixing with others outside the Church, whether for business or pleasure, we still keep our faith and all its implications 'shut in', for fear of being laughed at or politely ignored and put down as being odd or peculiar.

Yes, we behave as if Christ really was dead. We may roll back the stone and let him out when we are mixing with our fellow Christians, yet we hurriedly push him back and seal the stone in position before we set out among mankind at large. We shut the door to all the things we don't like and which threaten us. Yet Jesus comes and stands in our midst. He is not put off by our fears and compromises.

v.20　'Peace be with you,' he says; ending the tension which our tendency to look two ways at the same time sets up.

'Peace be unto you' is the characteristic resurrection greeting. It is kept vividly before us when we greet each other in the Eucharist, before we receive the risen life of Christ in the act of Holy Communion. Peace, unity, reconciliation, wholeness within, in place of the intolerable tensions which, when not faced up to, can lead to serious illness and mental sickness. We live in a state of warfare, so vividly experienced by St Paul who wrote, 'I fail to carry out the things I want to do, and I find myself doing the very things I hate' (Rom. 7:15). We bitterly resent our failures – things such as the fact that we are not sought after like others, that marriage has passed us by or that we are only attracted to members of our own sex, that we are envious, greedy, lazy, afraid of loneliness, sex-ridden and lusting after money. So often we find it difficult to live with ourselves. We are so bent on self-improvement and even imagine that this is what Christianity is about! We think we can save ourselves and that when we have repressed ourselves into the kind of person of whom God might approve, then we will bring to him the result of our self-culture and expect him to give us a pat on the back and shout 'Hurrah! Well done!'

We won't accept ourselves as we are. But God does. The kind of people Christ welcomes are those who accept themselves as they are – the penitent thief, the woman taken in adultery, Peter after his denial and the prodigal son who came back, not trying to put a good face on things but accepting his failure. We need a saviour for we cannot save ourselves, cannot pull ourselves up by our own shoe strings. We need a saviour who will take us as we are. We must learn how to forgive ourselves.

The peace the risen Lord wants to give us will completely elude us, so long as we go on pretending. Why must we pretend to ourselves that we are somebody else, trying to live up to the image of the 'perfect me'? It is an image of fantasy and an escape route from reality. Why must we pretend with others, presenting a façade? Because at any cost we want to be wanted, accepted, loved, cherished and envied. We cannot bear to be thought a failure, that my 'self' idol has toppled off its pedestal! Yet this was part of the experience of Christ as his popularity declined and the way of the cross opened up. We say that we want to be like him. So there can be no side-stepping of his pain.

How many marriages and, indeed, other close relationships, founder because in the beginning they are built up on façades and pretence? And, most foolish of all, we try to pretend with God. We polish up a nice little religious image of ourselves and present it to him for his approval. This is the game of self-righteousness. Into the midst of this tangle of tension the risen Lord says, 'Peace be with you.' Be at one, be whole within yourself, accept yourself.

'He . . . showed them his hands and his side'; the marks of sin, not his own, but that of mankind. We have to learn how to live with our own wounds. We shall never escape these marks, the fruit of our own self-will and of fear. The resurrection did not obliterate them. It transfigured them and we have to accept them and live with them if we would know peace. Peter is an interesting case to consider. He was certainly not prepared to accept the possibility of his own failure (Luke 22:31–34; Mark 14:26–31). But in the end he had to accept it. It was this acceptance of himself that was for him one of the great experiences of the resurrection. He had a private revelation of the risen Lord. Think what this must have meant to him (Luke 24:35). Perhaps, too, he had a moment of truth at the feet washing at the Last Supper. He began by thinking it was unnecessary, an affront to his self-respect. But then he suddenly stopped pretending and accepted his own need (John 13:2–11).

v.21 'As the Father sent me, so am I sending you.' Each time we receive the risen Christ in Holy Communion, he is saying, 'I am sending you.' We are, as Teresa of Avila says, his lips, his hands, his feet and his heart in the world today.

How can he make himself known and loved except through us, who are his body (the Church)?

vv.22–23 It is not without significance that this particular resurrection appearance is linked with the inauguration of the sacrament of penance (reconciliation). 'For those whose sins you forgive . . . etc'. It is through the use of this sacrament that we grow in the risen Lord's promise of peace. We cannot use it until we have accepted ourselves as we are and have, like the prodigal son, gone back to the Father, aware of our need and sure of our acceptance. Like all good things, this sacrament can be abused. Admitting to our failure with our neighbour in the confessional does not excuse us for not trying to put it right outside the confessional. One of the Christian characteristics is that we are supposed to love our neighbours as ourselves. The main cause for our differences with them is our non-acceptance of them. So often when we criticise or in some way try to destroy them it is because we see in them what we loathe to see in ourselves, but which is there. We say frequently 'forgive us our trespasses as we forgive those who trespass against us'. How can we do this unless we have really learned how to live with each other's failures, peculiarities, difficulties, obsessions and idiosyncrasies? When we can accept each other as we are, instead of trying to force and bully them into what we think they ought to be, we shall achieve some of that wholeness and unity which the risen Lord is wanting to give us through the use of the confessional.

Read slowly and reflectively John 20:19–23. Spend 30 minutes on this.

v.19 Do I live a shut-in, Church-centred life? What are my non-Church interests and associations?

v.20 'Peace be with you.' Write down on a sheet of paper who and what makes me tense and stressed. Why? Is there anyone with whom I am not reconciled? Am I appreciative of myself? Grateful for God's creation of me? Grateful for my talents? Do I have a right love of myself? Can I forgive my own failures? Am I trying to be somebody else in my relationship with God? Bringing to him and other people the kind of person I think I ought to be instead of the real me he created me to be? 'He . . . showed them his hands and his side.' We have to learn to live with our own wounds. What are my wounds?

v.23 The authority to pronounce absolution given to the disciples – the inauguration of the sacrament of reconciliation (confession). How often do I use this sacrament? Is there anyone with whom I am not reconciled? How do I accept those with whom I disagree?

Sit still for 15 minutes DOING NOTHING.

FOURTH MEDITATION

John 21:1–17.

v.1 Later on, Jesus showed himself again to the disciples. It was by the Sea of Tiberias, and it happened like this:

v.2 Simon Peter, Thomas called the Twin, Nathanael from Cana in Galilee, the sons of Zebedee and two more of his disciples were together.

v.3 Simon Peter said, 'I'm going fishing'. They replied, 'We'll come with you'. They went out and got into the boat but caught nothing that night.

v.4 It was light by now and there stood Jesus on the shore, though the disciples did not realise that it was Jesus.

v.5 Jesus called out, 'Have you caught anything, friends?'

v.6 And when they answered, 'No', he said, 'Throw the net out to starboard and you'll find something'. So they dropped the net, and there were so many fish that they could not haul it in.

v.7 The disciple Jesus loved said to Peter, 'It is the Lord'. At these words 'It is the Lord', Simon Peter, who had practically nothing on, wrapped his cloak round him and jumped into the water.

v.8 The other disciples came on in the boat, towing the net and the fish; they were only about a hundred yards from land.

v.9 As soon as they came ashore they saw that there was some bread there, and a charcoal fire with fish cooking on it.

v.10 Jesus said, 'Bring some of the fish you have just caught'.

v.11 Simon Peter went aboard and dragged the net to the shore, full of big fish, one hundred and fifty-three of them; and in spite of there being so many the net was not broken.

v.12 Jesus said to them, 'Come and have breakfast'. None of the disciples was bold enough to ask, 'Who are you?'; they knew quite well it was the Lord.

v.13 Jesus then stepped forward, took the bread and gave it to them, and the same with the fish.

v.14 This was the third time that Jesus showed himself to the disciples after rising from the dead.

v.15 After the meal Jesus said to Simon Peter, 'Simon son of John, do you love me more than these others do?' He answered, 'Yes Lord, you know I love you'. Jesus said to him, 'Feed my lambs'.

v.16 A second time he said to him, 'Simon son of John, do you love me?' He replied, 'Yes, Lord, you know I love you'. Jesus said to him, 'Look after my sheep'.

v.17 Then he said to him a third time, 'Simon son of John, do you love me?' Peter was upset that he asked him the third time, 'Do you love me?' and said, 'Lord, you know everything; you know I love you'. Jesus said to him, 'Feed my sheep'.

Reflection

vv.1–8 The first part is about the old familiar things. The disciples were at this stage uncertain of the future, so they tried to go back.

(1) To the Sea of Tiberias, Galilee, the old haunts.
(2) 'I'm going fishing,' said Peter.
(3) They caught nothing (which often happened).

Our Lord enters into this and going back to a similar situation in the past says, 'Throw the net out to starboard and you'll find something.' And again the result is the same as in the past, 'Peter went aboard and dragged the net to shore, full of big fish . . .'

vv.9–14 Our Lord is concerned about their bodily needs and has a meal waiting. So often in the past he was concerned when people were hungry . . . the feeding of the five thousand . . . etc. Supplying the needs of the hungry and starving has always been an important part of the Christian faith, so we must ask, 'What do I do about it?'

It is these old familiar things which make them sure that it is the risen Lord (as it was at Emmaus and also when Mary of Magdala was called by her name). We all have a tendency to like the old familiar things and sometimes we let ourselves be imprisoned by them. They have their place, but unless they lead on to new things, which the needs of our age require, we shall find ourselves living in a museum, in a valley of dry bones, fascinating, but DEAD. Our Lord is leading the disciples on from the familiar to their new future. He is not destroying tradition. He is enlarging it by deeper insights. The disciples are still to be fishermen, but their catch is to become men and women. Tradition is not about remaining the same. It is rather the sequence of present moments in which the Church responds with faith and fidelity to the word of God.

vv.15–17 The three questions to Peter balance his three denials after Our Lord's arrest. It is a kind of second call. The first had been by the Sea of Galilee (Mark 1:16–18). It involved a personal commitment to Our Lord.

Now the call is to more than a personal relationship; it is expanded into commitment to one's neighbour, 'Feed my lambs.' This reflects our own growth in the faith. At first when the truth of the Christian faith is revealed to us we are wholly absorbed in Christ. This can degenerate into a kind of hobby, a private cult, 'I keep my religion to myself and I won't have others interfering. It is too private.' But the Christian faith is not just a personal relationship between the individual and Christ. This is an essential and necessary feature of it, but Christianity is a relationship between persons. It is trinitarian; 'Feed my lambs, look after my sheep.'

I think we all receive a second call. It is when we suddenly or gradually realise that our Christian faith is not only churchgoing, not only beautiful and satisfying forms of worship, but that having met the risen Lord in worship we are to go out and feed and look after the sheep. The second call can take a variety of forms. It may be to create a Christian marriage and family life, it may be to be a priest or a monk or nun, to change our job or career and take on one which involves more direct service to others' needs, or to give more time to voluntary work in the Church or community. Whatever we do, we all have to ask ourselves, 'What am I doing about the sick, the lonely, the aged, the incapacitated, the housebound, the mentally ill, the orphan . . . etc?' What service are we giving them other than prayer?

Are we playing an active part in any non-religious organisation, political, recreational, educational . . . etc? We probably have not got the time to do more than one thing. But there should be something.

We must pray urgently for the grace to be really outgoing people, trying to accept people as they are. So often, without realising it, we stoop down in a condescending kind of way from our pedestals, arrogantly thinking we have all the answers. Yes, even self-righteousness can be totally sacrificial, but it is a sacrifice made to provide fuel for our own self-exaltation. In this kind of outgoing there is little seen of the warm humanity of Christ. St Paul puts it very succinctly: 'If I give away all that I possess, piece by piece, and if I even let them take my body to burn it, but am without love, it will do me no good whatever' (1 Cor. 13:3). Some will give themselves wholly to a good cause but it will be at the expense of parents, wives and children left at home to cope with what they themselves should be doing.

'Feed my lambs' does not mean setting out to improve people. There must be no strings attached to our efforts. We have to meet people on the level of their need. It means listening to them and discovering what a lot we have to learn from them St Paul says 'Rejoice with those who rejoice and be sad with those in sorrow' (Rom. 12:15). We may think that we are taking Christ to others, but he is already there before we arrive. We are all created in the image of God and the Spirit of God dwells within each one of us, although often unrecognised and denied. We are to look for and love Jesus in others. People are often suspicious of our help and friendship; they think we are going to exact a price in the end, that we are really looking out for converts and not loving and serving them purely for their own sake. Yet Christ loves them for themselves and endures the pain of their not realising it. We have to share that.

It is sad that Christians have the reputation of being so condemning and unaccepting of people today who have got themselves entangled in the contemporary webs of sexual freedom, marital confusion, the cults of money, drugs, fear, doubt and meaninglessness. Sometimes we set out eagerly to serve, but then we get disappointed, bored and frustrated because those we serve and befriend don't seem to change. They are entangled and addicted to their difficulties, obsessions and fecklessness. It is just these we have to accept. Remember, Our Lord said, 'I was in prison and you came to see me ... etc' (Matt. 25:35–40) ... and still in prison when we left them and still waiting to be visited again! Don't forget St Paul's advice to us, 'Love ... is always ready to excuse, to trust, to hope, and to endure whatever comes' (1 Cor. 13:7).

We must be accepting of people and then the attractiveness of Christ will shine through us. We want to be able to say, as Peter did, 'Lord you know everything, you know I love you'. But the test is seen in Our Lord's reply, 'Feed my sheep' (John 21:17). We know how Our Lord feeds us in the Eucharist, the bread of life and the cup of salvation. This touch of the resurrection. Each communion is a meeting with the same risen Lord whom Peter met by the shore of the lake. He feeds us that we may feed others. How fortunate we are if we have the time and opportunity to feed daily on the heavenly manna, the bread of life, the body of Christ ... we should do so as often as we can. 'Give us this day our daily bread.'

Read slowly and reflectively again John 21:1–17. Spend 30 minutes on this.

The first part is about returning to the old familiar things. What things? Do I indulge in nostalgia for the past? The Christian life is a pilgrimage, a continual looking forward to heaven – we have here no abiding city. What kind of thoughts and images come into my mind when I think of heaven?

Read Matthew 25:35–46.

In what ways do I serve my neighbour in his/her need? Do I expect results from serving my neighbour? Am I accepting of them? Or always wanting to improve them! We have to make 1 Corinthians 13 part of ourselves if we are to give ourselves to others without looking for some kind of return.

Read reflectively 1 Corinthians 13.

Sit still for 15 minutes DOING NOTHING.

II. A Retreat on the Triumph of the Cross and Passion

Much of the thinking in the First Meditation on the mystery of evil is the fruit of discussion with the late Archbishop Trevor Huddleston, C.R., when he was preparing his mission to Oxford University.

FIRST MEDITATION

The mystery of evil.

To be confronted with the passion and death of Christ is to come face to face with the mystery of evil. Every generation becomes aware of the force of evil. In our own day the TV news is largely a record of the world's sins. The banner headlines and long columns in newspapers are mostly accounts of evil and its effects. The list seems endless. Wars setting man against man, race against race, the confrontation of ideologies, torture, genocide, terror and violence, starvation and homelessness on a vaster scale than ever before in the history of the world, the threat of reducing the world to a heap of atomic ash, the demise of marriage, the misuse of creation, the destruction of the environment, the thickening fog of fear, the suffocation of materialism, the dying of the Western world because people are trying to live through bread alone.

There are two accounts of the origin of evil in the Bible.

1) The cosmic account. Evil came to birth in the spiritual world of the angels, before ever the earth existed. Satan, the devil, was once Lucifer, the Angel of Light. But he grew envious and would be as God. So there was war in heaven.

   'And now war broke out in heaven, when Michael and his angels attacked the dragon. The dragon fought back with his angels, but they were defeated and driven out of heaven. The great dragon, the primeval serpent, known as the devil or Satan, who had deceived all the world, was hurled down to the earth and his angels were hurled down with him' (Rev. 12:7–9).

Evil is not just something which springs up in our relationships with each other. This account says the origin of evil is outside time and space (angels and spirits), outside human measurement and experience. This is what St Paul believed and so he wrote, 'For it is not against human enemies that we have to struggle, but against the Sovereignties and the Powers who originate the darkness in this world, the spiritual army of evil in the heavens' (Eph. 6:12).

If evil is in our environment, perhaps it helps us to see dimly why nations and races can behave so destructively towards each other, when in fact the greater number of those on either side have nothing against each other as individuals. It is easy to believe there is evil or darkness in an environment if one has encountered witchcraft or been in certain places which are said to be 'haunted'. Dogs, too, are sensitive to atmosphere and the guard dogs at the Tower of London cannot be persuaded to enter the White Tower there.

2) The other account of the origin of evil is in the story of Adam and Eve (Gen. 3). This tries to explain why evil exists between people in their relationships with each other. Evil comes from within us. Our Lord spoke of this, 'It is what comes out of a man that makes him unclean. For it is from within, from men's hearts, that evil intentions emerge: fornication, . . . malice, deceit, indecency, envy, slander, pride, folly. All these evil things come from within and make a man unclean' (Mark 7:21–23). We are capable of making the right choices, but we often choose

the opposite. We have heavenly aspirations but we grovel around in the dustbins and cesspits. We are capable of love but we often prefer lust.

So, one account of evil limits it to man, to his divided heart, and the other makes it a cosmic matter. The truth probably lies in both. But in each account the origin of evil is due to disobedience and the consequences are deprivation, separation and death. If the solution to the problem of evil simply depended on our goodwill, then Christ need only have been a moral teacher and the energies and efforts of the great religious men of history would have solved it – Mohammed, Buddha, Gandhi, etc. But we have not solved it. We know it to be a problem and a mystery overwhelming us NOW.

Why do we twist and misuse good things so that the result is grief, division and disaster? Why is it that we in the Western world have more than enough of the good things of creation while the greater part has less than the bare necessities of existence? Nationalism can be such a good positive creative force in the development of a country, but the millions of graves scattered across Europe, the silent gas chambers of Auschwitz and Buchenwald, the ashes of Hiroshima and the unceasing streams of refugees show what evil can do with nationalism. Today Jew faces Arab in bitter confrontation and life is cheap in the Balkans and in so many other parts of the world.

There is nothing evil in scientific investigation and technological development. It is a growing knowledge of the amazing wonder of God's creation. Yet we misuse that knowledge. Is nuclear energy going to better our quality of life or destroy it altogether? Is psychiatry to be used to cure or to manipulate? The right use of drugs is marvellous for the sick, but look at the devastating effects of their misuse.

And finally there is death. To many it is the greatest disaster of all, to Christians the gateway to life. Everything we may achieve on a worldly level seems to end in futility. Our careers founder on the rocks of retirement and old age. The work of our hands falls into disrepair. The relationships we have so carefully built up are demolished by death. Our money and our possessions have to be left to others who will probably use them in ways which would disappoint us. But as Christians we can snap our fingers amidst the clouds of despair and doubt with which the power of evil seeks to suffocate the act of dying. We have always known and lived as if we had here no abiding city. We are seeking the one which is to come in the wonder of heaven.

Self-examination on how the shadow of evil may slant across you and obscure the vision of God

Don't rush this. Ponder each question reflectively. Write down the answers as to what the Holy Spirit is saying to you.

* Do you pray for others, that God's will be done by them, realising that it may be contrary to what you think is best for them?
* Is your eucharistic worship regular and are you grateful for God's gift of himself in Holy Communion?
* Have you selfishly refused to help someone in need when you could have done, 'passing by on the other side'?
* Do you have a plan about almsgiving? What is it? How does it compare with what you spend on yourself?

- Are you prepared to lend to others and would you be ruthless about demanding repayment?
- Do you give only when you expect something in return?
- Do you keep your home to yourself or is it a place of open hospitality?
- Have you cold-shouldered anyone or tried to exclude them?
- Are you generous in affirming, praising and supporting others or are you silent and inwardly envious and outwardly critical because they have gifts you would like to have?
- How do you relate to those in grief or trouble?
- Do you like to control and dominate people and situations, never delegating responsibilities or giving people the opportunity for self-expression?
- Do you try to stamp down on the growth of your husband/wife because you are afraid to cope with change?
- Who do you take for granted? If so, why?

SECOND MEDITATION

Matthew 26:36–46; Mark 14:32–42; Luke 22:39–46 (Gethsemane).

The Christian faith has never claimed that evil is not a mystery. But we confront the mystery of evil with the mystery of Gethsemane, Golgotha and the empty tomb. We realise that we cannot save ourselves. The history of the human race, especially in recent times, is the tragic history of those who think they can. Christians don't know why there is evil, but we do believe it can be conquered by all that we commemorate from Palm Sunday to Easter Day. God has provided a way whereby we can meet evil, meet its consequences and grow more Christ-like. Instead of being swamped by fear and drowned in self-pity, we can meet the last evil of death singing with St Paul, 'Death is swallowed up in victory. Death, where is your victory? Death, where is your sting? Now the sting of death is sin, and sin gets its power from the Law. So let us thank God for giving us the victory through our Lord Jesus Christ' (1 Cor. 15:54–57).

It was in Gethsemane that Our Lord confronted the whole force of evil, taking it upon himself and becoming sin for us. 'The sins of the world rushed upon him.' What does this mean? Alas! He had to bear what is well known to us, what is familiar to us. He had to bear the backslidings and evil

I am indebted to Cardinal John Henry Newman for much of the reflection on the meaning of Gethsemane.

deeds, so welcome, so easy, and so dear to us, but which to
him had the scent and the poison of death. Sin is so easy a
thing to us. We think little of it. We do not understand how
God can think much of it. We cannot even bring ourselves
to believe it deserves punishment. We are always ready to
explain it away and we hate being told about it. But it is
a rebellion against God and our neighbour; it is always
destructive. It is the mortal enemy of the ALL HOLY.

So, because Our Lord had taken on himself our human
nature, sin sought to take possession of him. And in that
most awful hour he knelt in Gethsemane, dismissing his
reluctant angels who in their thousands were ready at
his call, and opening his arms and baring his breast, sinless
as he was, he met the full assault of the foe, whose breath
was a pestilence and whose embrace was agony.

We are told, 'And sadness came over him, and great distress' (Matt. 26:37). There he knelt motionless and still,
while the vile and horrible fiend clung close around his
heart, filling every corner of his being, until he felt himself
to be that which he could never be, but which sin hoped he
would be.

We are told, 'In his anguish he prayed even more earn-
estly, and his sweat fell to the ground like great drops of
blood' (Luke 22:44). Oh, the horror when he looked and did
not know himself and felt himself to be a foul and loathsome
sinner. Oh, the distraction when he felt his eyes, his hands,
his feet, his heart, as if belonging to the evil one and not to
God. Are these the hands of the sinless Son of God which
now feel themselves red with ten thousand deeds of blood?
Are these his lips, not uttering prayer and praise, but defiled
with oaths and blasphemies? And his eyes are blinded by
all the evil visions and fascinations for which men and
women have cast God on one side. His ears are ringing with

revelry and strife and his heart is frozen with greed and cruelty and unbelief and his very memory is laden with every sin that has been committed from the beginning of time to the end of the world.

Which of us does not know the misery of a haunting thought which comes again and again? Of destructive criticism which leaps out in spite of all our efforts to beat it back? Of despair which engulfs and envy which gnaws daily at the heart? And these gather round thee, blessed Lord, in millions now. They come in troops and battle array. The sins of the living and the dead and of those yet to be born. The sins of the lost and the saved. The sins of sinners and of saints. They are all there. All but one.

Only one is not there; one only; for she had no part in sin. She could only console him and she is not there. She will be at his side at the cross, but she is separated from him in the garden. For thirty years she was his mother at Nazareth, but her virgin ear and her pure heart cannot understand the evil that is on him now.

Only God can bear the weight of such sin. It is the long tragic history of the world.

- Hopes blighted.
- The scramble for money.
- The bewitching of the consumer society.
- Vows broken.
- Warnings scorned.
- Opportunities lost.
- Vocations cast on one side.
- The innocent betrayed.
- The young hardened.
- The penitent falling back into sin.
- The just overcome.

- The aged failing.
- The arrogance of those who deny God.
- The abandonment to sexual lust and passion.
- The slime of the misuse of sex.
- The pornography industry.
- The canker of remorse.
- The endless worrying.
- The quest for snobbery and position.
- The anguish of shame.
- The pining of disappointment.
- The sickness of despair.
- The cries of concentration camps.
- The streams of refugees.
- The sighs of the starving.
- The hopelessness of the displaced.
- The ashes of Hiroshima.
- The racial discrimination.
- The silent screams of the aborted.

Such cruel, heartrending, revolting and despicable scenes. They are all before him now; they are upon him and in him. They are with him in the place of that peace which until now has reigned in his heart. He cries to the Father as if he were the criminal and not the victim, 'He threw himself on the ground and prayed that, if it were possible, this hour might pass from him' (Mark 14:35).

He is doing penance for us: he is making confession for us. He is the satisfaction for the sins of the world. 'And yet ours were the sufferings he bore, ours the sorrows he carried' (Isa. 53:4). He rose. He lifted his face for the traitor's kiss and lo! there is blood upon his brow, blood trickling down his garments, blood staining the brown earth. But whence comes this blood? The scourge has not touched him yet. The thorns have not bit into his brow nor the nails torn his hands and feet. He has bled before his time. He has shed blood and it is the agony in his soul which has sent it forth; the agony of the All Holy taking on himself the mystery of evil. His passion has begun within. His heart, usually so full of love and peace, is tormented. It begins to labour and to beat quicker and quicker, 'the fountains of the great deep were broken up'. The red streams poured forth so fast and fierce, that they overflowed the veins and bursting through the pores of his skin formed into great drops which fell to the ground staining the brown earth.

He has accepted the mystery of evil, though his whole being is fraught with fear and revulsion. '"Father", he said, "if you are willing, take this cup away from me. Nevertheless, let your will be done, not mine"' (Luke 22:42). They are words which will lead up to Calvary, down to the grave and into the wonder of the resurrection. Are they words we have written into our own lives?

Self-examination on how the mystery of evil may seek to entwine you and obscure the vision of God.

Write down your answers to these questions:

1) Do you take delight in others' failings and misfortunes?
2) Are you quick to judge and condemn, in spite of your own many failings?
3) Are you quick to admit your mistakes and wrongs and seek forgiveness?
4) Are you touchy about criticism and quick to take offence?

5) Do you enjoy drawing attention to yourself? Have you shown priggishness, complacency or smugness?

6) Does pride prevent you exposing your needs and vulnerability to others?

7) Have you been too dependent on others and made life difficult for them?

8) Do you try to bully and manipulate others by your moods?

9) As a husband/wife do you really love and cherish each other, growing in trust and acceptance of each other, and always ready to say sorry when you have done something to injure the relationship?

10) As a parent have you been truly loving, fair and firm with your children, praying with them, and bringing them up in the faith?

11) If unmarried have you entered into the wrong kind of emotional relationship with someone who is already married? Do you regard sex as a plaything and encourage casual encounters?

12) If a celibate, do you seek out friendship and service which your freedom from marriage makes possible? Have you compromised your celibacy by any sexual involvement? Have you withdrawn into a condemning kind of prudishness or the wrong kind of isolation?

13) If a homosexual, have you accepted yourself or are you full of resentment? Have you been sexually promiscuous? Do you discuss the fidelity and the sacrifice involved in trying to create a permanent partnership with someone? Is it the kind of partnership which is truly in Christ?

THIRD MEDITATION

Incidents on the way of the cross.

The passion and sufferings of Christ are always with us. They are not just something that happened a long time ago. Their causes are always with us. Our Lord told us that whatever we do to anyone we do it to him NOW (Matt. 25:31–46). The Press, the TV and the radio plunge us into the Stations of the Cross. They present us with the opportunity for a deeper union with Christ. We can, of course, let the tragedies and sufferings of the world come between us and God and almost destroy our belief in him, instead of finding there Christ in his passion and on his cross. Suffering is the only way into the heart of God. We, the baptised, are his Body on earth now so he is crucified afresh whenever we behave with cruelty to each other. We would like to think that we are always on the side of Christ. Alas! We know that is not always so.

1) Christ before Pilate (Matt. 27:1–26; Mark 15:1–15; Luke 23:2–7, 13–25; John 18:28—19:16).

Here is the man Pilate sitting in judgement on God. The creature judging the Creator, as if the car said to the driver, 'I am in charge of speed and direction.' Do we sit in judgement with Pilate, trying to make God unnecessary and push him out of our lives? We think that we have got the world under control; technology will support us and we are making a bid for space. If we do have any personal problems or difficulties we go to the psychiatrist's couch to smooth them out. So do we condemn him with Pilate? God is needed no more and grace is only autosuggestion. We want to get rid of Christ. He makes uncomfortable, demanding claims which seem to be in conflict with the fashion of the day. So 'away with him, crucify him'.

Pilate washed his hands of the matter. This outward action deceived no one, least of all himself. He was evading his responsibilities. He was clinging to the security of his position. He did not want to lose his job. It would not further his ambition if reports reached Rome that he had unnecessarily stirred up trouble with the Jews, who were a troublesome lot anyway and did not sit lightly under Roman occupation. But no one is deceived. And we are like Pilate. We won't take the blame for our own failings. We can always find an excuse. A broken marriage and each is convinced it's the other's fault. It's because of my parents, my boss, my job, my health – anything but me! We wash our hands of every situation. The starving of the world, the racial tensions in our society, the lonely old woman down the street, the man just out of prison. Someone ought to do something. But not me. I'm not interfering. Or are we like Pilate and don't want to offend those in authority over us? We don't want to spoil our chances of promotion, or lose friends, so we hold our tongues; we cling to our worldly security. Time after time, both as individuals and as a Church, we have compromised, preferring worldly prestige to truth and mercy. Pilate is alive and well in us!

2) Christ falls beneath the weight of the cross

on the way to Calvary and Simon from Cyrene is dragged out from the crowd to carry it for him (Luke 23:26).

Traditionally Christ fell beneath the cross three times. The weight of the cross is the weight of sin. The world (the cult of money and possessions), the flesh (the cult of the body) and the devil (the cult of self-will) are the three things we renounced at baptism. So Christ staggers beneath them.

(i) *The world*. The society in which we live is obsessed with money. This is inflamed by the lottery, the many quizzes and competitions for glittering prizes. So much sleaze has to do with bribes and 'handouts'. The whole world of advertising is geared to persuading us to buy more and more things, telling us constantly that luxuries are essentials. The pressures are enormous. Do you want to be beautiful and attractive and desirable? Buy a bottle of this or a tube of that. Do you want a happy home? Nothing but the largest TV screen will do. Do you want security? It's impossible without insurance. Do you want the neighbours to stare? A new sleek car standing outside the door will do the trick. It is difficult not to be ensnared. Yet while we crave for more and more things, half the world is dying of starvation and the poor get poorer. It is not wrong to have money, to earn it or to win it. The crucial question is, what do we do with it? Serve ourselves or our neighbour? For false profits and greed Christ falls. It is part of our twisted nature to misuse money.

(ii) *The flesh*. Was any society ever so obsessed with sex as ours? It is the worship of the goddess Venus. All day

long our sexual desires are stimulated by advertisements, glossy magazines, films and plays, the TV screen
and the explicit details of people's sexual lives in the
Press. For the Christian, sexual acts should imply commitment, trust, tenderness, respect for the other and
the desire for an on-going, responsible, faithful, lifelong
communion with each other. Such acts are meant to be
enjoyed. For many today sex is just for fun, a plaything
to be grabbed or bought at any opportunity. It is lust
let loose. The body is the temple of the Holy Spirit and
there are many other ways of misusing it. We abuse it
with drugs and over-eating (the quantity of different
foods and drinks the advertisements tell us we need
is infinite). The god of the body is exercised in the
gymnasium, worshipped obsessively by slimming and
ministered to by the health food stores, vitamin addiction and finally the plastic surgeon.

(iii) *The devil.* Here we come to the heart of the tragedy of
the human race. It is disobedience. The story of Adam
and Eve is an attempt to explain how defying our
Creator brings disaster. We serve ourselves at the
expense of others and this gives birth to hatred, division, exploitation and the misuse of creation. Mary's
obedience in accepting the invitation of God to be the
mother of Christ is in sharp contrast to Eve's disobedience. Christ is perfectly obedient to the will of the
Father in order to undo what we have knotted. Obedience is the keynote of his life. The first recorded words
from his lips at the age of twelve are spoken to his
mother and St Joseph, when they had lost him and
eventually found him in the Temple, in religious discussion with the doctors. In response to their agitation
he replied, 'Did you not know that I must be busy with

my Father's affairs?' (Luke 2:49). And again, later in his public life, 'I always do what pleases him' (John 8:29), and again, 'I have come from heaven, not to do my own will, but to do the will of the one who sent me' (John 6:38). Finally, in the garden of Gethsemane, 'Nevertheless, let your will be done, not mine' (Luke 22:43). Our obedience to God should, like Christ's, shine out from our lives. Our Lord calls us to be the light of the world (Matt. 5:14–16).

The three falls beneath the weight of the world, the flesh, and the devil are the three opposites of poverty, chastity and obedience. The latter are the outstanding characteristics of the life of Our Lord and we have to come to terms with them. We are fully implicated in these falls. We are not just spectators. So we have to reflect on our use of things, our use of our bodies and our wills. Ask ourselves too whether God is calling us to a rather specialised acceptance of poverty, chastity and obedience within the framework of the monastery or convent.

There is much talk today about self-fulfilment. We're told that we have to be OURSELVES even at other people's expense and inconvenience. Is there a conflict between our obedience to God and self-fulfilment? Reflect on what you mean by self-fulfilment in the circumstances of your own life. Does it seem thwarted by the claims of Christ? What is true self-fulfilment? Is it possible without suffering?

Simon the Cyrenian was a black man. His being compelled to assist Our Lord plunges us immediately into all the issues of racialism and of ethnic cleansing. Penitence for the black slave trade of the past is not enough. How do we react to the multi-racial society in which we live, particularly when it means competition in the work force or when our daughters and sons contract inter-racial marriages?

More searching questions about following the Way of Christ

Write down the answers.

(1) Are you ready to forgive others and seek reconciliation with those who have become alienated from you?

(2) Are you trusting after reconciliation or do you make terms and keep the other 'on trial'?

(3) Do you bear grudges and nurse feelings?

(4) Do you dwell on old conflicts from the past and reopen old wounds?

(5) Do you write people off as hopeless because you have become dissatisfied with them?

(6) Do you stay faithful in friendships, accepting the crises and differences which may occur, with patience?

(7) Have you ever tried to seek revenge?

(8) Have you made anyone into a scapegoat?

(9) Do you wash your hands of people or stereotype them and then are you not prepared to meet them? Do you act as if the Holy Spirit could not change people?

(10) Are you prepared to accept other people's opinions peacefully or do you want to mould them into what you think is the 'right shape'?

(11) Do you demand your own perfectionism of others?

FOURTH MEDITATION

The Holy Cross.

Each year on September the fourteenth the Church keeps the Feast of the Triumph of the Cross. It is a day of thanksgiving for all the cross means to Christians. It would, of course, have no meaning at all if Jesus had not risen from the dead. If his crumbling bones are still lying somewhere beneath the streets of Jerusalem, his crucifixion becomes just one more act of gross injustice, inflicted by those who found him both a political and religious threat. There have been many such martyrs to injustice throughout the history of the human race. But Jesus rose again, both body and soul, from the tomb. Therefore, at once, the cross becomes transformed and bathed in the golden light of love, and so we fashion this horrific instrument of suffering and death in gold and silver and ivory and stud it with precious jewels. Every skill of the artist, the sculptor and the carver is brought to bear on it. We refer to it in hymns as 'sweetest wood' and the nails as 'sweetest iron' and say 'sweetest weight is hung on thee'.

The cross has become the sign and symbol of Christianity. We put it both inside and outside our church buildings. We nail the crucifix on the walls of our homes. We wear it hanging round our necks. It glows invisibly and indelibly on our foreheads where we were marked with it at baptism. We constantly make the sign of the cross on ourselves when we pray and when we worship. Volumes and volumes of books have been written and will continue to be written about what God has done for us through the crucifixion of Jesus, his Son. We use religious and theological words such as redemption, salvation, atonement and reconciliation in trying to understand the mystery of what God has done for us through the cross of Jesus. Like all the mysteries of the Christian faith it can never be fathomed by our finite minds nor adequately expressed in words. The simplest words perhaps best convey what we sense instinctively. So we sing in the familiar hymn,

> There is a green hill far away . . .
> He died that we might be forgiven.
> He died to make us good.
> That we might go at last to heaven
> Saved by his precious blood.
> There was no other good enough
> To pay the price of sin.
> He only could unlock the gate of heaven
> And let us in.

So we can begin to catch glimpses of what St Paul meant when he wrote 'The only thing I can BOAST about is the cross of our Lord Jesus Christ, through whom the world is crucified to me, and I to the world' (Gal. 6:14). Christians, belonging to the body of Christ on earth, know what it is to be crucified with Christ by the times in which we live.

- We are crucified by the drug culture.
- We are crucified by the avalanche of abortions and the cult of euthanasia.
- We are crucified by the multitude of broken marriages, broken homes and unwanted and abused children.
- We are crucified by the cult of money and materialistic goals.
- We are crucified by the addiction to sex.

- We are crucified by the violence on our streets.
- We are crucified by the manufacture and proliferation of land mines throughout the world.
- We are crucified by our misuse of the environment God has created for us.
- We are crucified by our own sense of helplessness in stemming the waves of secularism which engulf us.

We cannot, however, separate ourselves from the society in which we live. We are all part of it and 'no man is an island'. We all share the responsibility for what has come upon us. We are all totally dependent on each other and we are our 'brother's keeper'. To enter the supermarket is to be overwhelmed by the choice of foods. When we purchase them we become linked with all those who have worked to produce them for us. We switch on the electric light and at once we are caught up with all those who make it possible for us to enjoy such a convenience. We may feel crucified by the thinking and behaviour of those on whom we are so dependent but at the same time we are linked with them in being the crucifiers too. We are on both sides of the fence!

We gaze at the crucifix. We look at the hands of Christ . . . those hands which touched the eyes of the blind, those hands which lifted up the lame, those hands which healed the leper and were laid in blessing on the heads of children, those hands which washed the feet of the disciples and held the bread and the cup at the Last Supper. Why should they now be fastened, held and torn by the nails? Because we have been so free with our hands. Free to strike the angry blow, free to fiddle the books and take what does not belong to us, free to do our work carelessly or to fold them in idleness and refuse to help those in need. For this freedom his hands are fastened.

We look at the feet of Christ . . . those feet which walked on the waters of the lake, those feet which carried him up the mountain to pray and be transfigured, those feet which carried him to so many places to bring blessings and a new understanding of God. Why should they now be fastened, held and torn by the nails? Because we have been so free with our feet to turn away from God and his Church, free to walk away from our husbands, our wives and our children, free to walk through the divorce courts or into the abortion clinic, free to visit people and places which we knew would cause us and others trouble and unhappiness. For this freedom his feet are fastened.

We look at the mouth and lips of Christ . . . they are cracked and parched with thirst. He can scarcely speak . . . those lips which had spoken the truth about God's love for us, brought us blessings where there had been despair, health where there had been sickness, light where there had been darkness, understanding where there had been confusion and peace where there had been strife. Why should he now suffer such pain in speaking? Because we have been so free with our lips in letting forth a torrent of spite and slander, a spate of lies and temper, a flood of grumbling and growling, of innuendo and flattery. For this freedom he suffers thirst.

We gaze at his heart . . . it is the heart of God longing for some response to his great love for us, his longing to enfold us in his peace. Yet this heart, so full of love for every man, woman and child, is broken, pierced by the soldier's spear. Why should his heart be pierced and broken? Because our hearts are stuffed with self-love, self-pleasing, self-gratification, self-pity, self-choosing, self, self, self . . .

How can we respond? Flee to the confessional. God in his mercy has given us the sacrament of reconciliation. This sacrament is Our Lord's Easter gift to us because he waited until he had risen from the tomb before giving his disciples the authority to forgive sins (John 20:21–23). In the presence of God's priest we pour out all the ways in which we have been involved in Our Lord's crucifixion and then Our Lord speaking through the lips of his priest says, 'I forgive you.' We get up from our knees; we have died to the past and risen to a new beginning. God is so generous because by using this sacrament we can continue to make those essential new beginnings on our pilgrimage to heaven.

A final look at ourselves

(1) Have I been dishonest about showing my true feelings and deceived others by not speaking up?

(2) Have I behaved towards others with condescension or arrogance or argued just for the sake of stirring up trouble?

(3) Have I been mistrustful or suspicious of those I live and work and worship with?

(4) Have I been irresponsible or unfaithful in my obligations?

(5) Have I failed in my duties through carelessness, or delay or failed to do my fair share of work?

(6) Are there any promises I have not kept?

(7) Have I been a good steward of what has been entrusted to me, or have I been wasteful and extravagant?

Say slowly and reflectively ten times:

'As for me, the only thing I can boast about is the cross of Our Lord Jesus Christ, through whom the world is crucified to me, and I to the world' (Gal. 6:14). We adore you, O Christ, and we bless you because by your holy cross you have redeemed the world.

III. Going into Retreat with Mary

FIRST MEDITATION

The silence of Mary.

'As for Mary, she treasured all these things and pondered them in her heart' (Luke 2:19). 'His mother stored up all these things in her heart' (Luke 2:51). Mary is a woman of silence. So she is a good companion to have in the silence of a retreat. You are going to gaze with her on the mystery of God, Father, Son and Holy Spirit. Silence is the sound of God.

In the gospels we hear Mary speak only four times.

(1) Her question, when asked to be the mother of Jesus, 'how can this come about, since I am a virgin?' (Luke 1:34). Is God asking something of you which you feel is quite impossible?

(2) Her acceptance, 'I am the handmaid of the Lord,' said Mary 'let what you have said be done to me' (Luke 1:38). She took an enormous risk. Do you take risks for God?

(3) Her instructions to the waiters at the wedding reception at Cana, when, being a very observant person, she noticed the wine was running out. Pointing to Jesus she said to them, 'Do whatever he tells you' (John 2:5). It reads as if she almost forced the hand of Jesus. It is interesting too to note that this very first miracle of Jesus was so that people could have a good time. 'Do whatever he tells you,' is the keynote of Mary's life.

Can you say it is the keynote of your life? If not, why not?

(4) Mary's great song of joy and gladness (the Magnificat) when she visited her cousin Elizabeth (Luke 1:46–55). Mary was above all things a woman of gratitude. Is gratitude the keynote of your life?

Otherwise Mary is a silent figure. After her initial 'yes' to God her life was ordinary and unspectacular. She was no preacher. She stayed at home during most of Our Lord's public ministry. She was not a leader. In the early days of the Church she stayed in the background, totally involved in that most silent and yet most essential of operations, the work of prayer. A work of true 'mothering' (Acts 1:14).

However, since her reception into heaven and throughout the Christian centuries, she has broken her silence and God has sent her to speak to us. In the many Marian shrines throughout the world such as Lourdes, Fatima, Medjugorje, Guadeloupe, Knock and countless others, some people (often children) have had an 'experience' (vision) of Mary. She has brought messages from heaven. She says we are to reflect more and more on the meaning of the life of Jesus (the prayer of the rosary), we are to fast and pray more fervently and do what he tells us. All this is advice straight from the gospels and absolutely essential if the world is to be saved from destroying itself. Mary is still mothering us.

How are you going to take the silence of Mary into your retreat? Don't use it to talk to yourself in the way in which you talk to others, chattering, arguing, quarrelling, and justifying yourself to them in your own mind, even when they are not there. Wait, listen to the silence. Don't expect any unusual experience. Don't pour yourself out in self-accusation, beating your own breast. This is a form of self-indulgence. Allow yourself to meet yourself in the silence. Some will only let themselves meet themselves as they think they ought to be! Try to meet yourself as you are. Perhaps this will give you a terrible feeling. It may make you realise how remote all the people are with whom you are dealing every day; with whom you may even live and to whom you are supposed to be bound by ties of love. Perhaps you will feel nothing but a sinister feeling of emptiness and nothing. The psalmist says: 'I have kept silence, but it was pain and grief to me.' So others have been there before you. Bear with yourself. Again the psalmist says: 'Commune with your own heart and in your chamber and be still.' You may be aware of a great void. Listen to the silence. At first you will hear a variety of background noises, depending on where you are ... traffic, a dog barking, distant talking, the sound of the heating system etc. Plunge beneath all this. Listen to the silence deep down within yourself. You may feel surrounded on all sides by a great distance.

Do not yet call it God. It is only what points to God and by its namelessness and limitlessness, tells us that God is something other than just one more thing added to all those we usually have to deal with. It makes us aware of God's presence, if we are still and do not flee in terror from the mystery which is present and prevails in the silence. Don't flee from it in your mind, to the familiar haunts of your personal problems and anxieties.

This is only a beginning, a preparation for God to come in his fullness. It is the disposition of Mary before the archangel Gabriel was sent to her (Luke 1:26–28). It is a silence which cries out; it is both fear of death and the promise of the infinity which is near to us in blessing. And

these are too close together and too similar for us of ourselves to be able to interpret this infinity which is so remote
and yet so close.

This is the message of Mary; the message of the
incarnation . . . that God is so close to us, just where we are,
if we open up to this infinity. His remoteness then becomes
'presence' . . . unfathomable but yet pervading all things. He
is there with tender affection. He says, 'Do not be afraid'
(just as Gabriel said to Mary). He is within, inside this
prison of ourselves. Trust in this close presence. It is not
emptiness. Cast off what is holding you back and you will
find: 'Anyone who loses his life for my sake will find it'
(Matt. 10:39).

Eternity is descending into time; infinity into the finite.
God is making marriage with you . . . with each one of us,
and this festival is what the theologians aridly call 'grace'. It
takes place when we are still and wait . . . believing, hoping,
loving . . .

God became man, once in time, and ever since has gone
on doing so in you. Perhaps you think wrongly of the
incarnation, as a kind of disguising of God. If so, then God
remains purely and simply God and you would be uncertain
as to whether he is really here, where you are now. But God
is man. This does not mean he has ceased to be God in the
measureless plenitude of his glory. God is man. What is
human about him really says something about God and not
just something about us. Jesus is true man, a finite, free
human being, obediently accepting the unfathomable
mystery of his being. He accepted this and so you can dare
call out with him to God 'Father'. The word 'Father' is one
you can understand. It removes some of the incomprehensi-
bility of God. He is no longer remote. He is a measureless,

merciful presence. For he is both God and man: giver, gift and reception, call and answer in one.

Silence is an experience of what is infinite in your finite being. This experience is only possible because God the infinite became finite man in Christ. It is the experience of Mary. It gave her a self-awareness which would have been a totally different experience if God had not become man in her.

If you accept the silent, tremendous reality which surrounds you as if at a remote distance, yet at the same time close and overwhelming, if you accept it as a saving presence and a tender unreserved love, if you have the courage to understand yourself in a way which can only be done in grace and faith, then you will begin to penetrate the meaning of the phrase, 'The word was made flesh and dwelt among us.' And the words of the Te Deum, 'When you took our nature to save mankind you did not shrink from birth in the Virgin's womb.' And the words, 'How silently, how silently the wondrous gift is given.'

SECOND MEDITATION

Mary shares our own experiences.

Let Mary, the Mother of God, take you by the hand into this retreat. She is a good companion and guide, because she will take us straight to Jesus and whisper in our ear, as she did to those waiters at the wedding reception in Cana so long ago, 'Do whatever he tells you' (John 2:5).

Try to be as open to the promptings of the Holy Spirit as she was at her annunciation when she accepted God's invitation to be the mother of his son (Luke 1:38). Keep a spirit of gratitude and thanksgiving. In spite of problems and perplexities Mary sang, 'My soul proclaims the greatness of the Lord and my spirit exults in God my Saviour' (Luke 1:46).

Mary gives you a perfect description of what your retreat is about. When she was faced with bewildering, unexpected facts of having to give birth in a stable and act as hostess to shepherds and Wise Men, we are told twice by St Luke, 'As for Mary, she treasured all these things and pondered them in her heart', and 'His mother stored up all these things in her heart' (Luke 2:19, 52). Is not this a perfect description of what you are trying to do in this retreat? Perhaps you may have to face in the silence of your retreat what Mary had to face at the presentation in the Temple, when the aged Simeon said to her, 'A sword will pierce your own soul too' (Luke 2:35). What is your sword? Have you many sufferings to bear? Whose fault are they?

Mary fled into exile into Egypt (Matt. 2:13–14). It was forced upon her through no fault of her own. She did not enjoy the experience of being a refugee. It may be that your retreat will be an exile experience, when God seems to desert you. You came into retreat to find him and all you can cry out is 'My God, my God, why have you deserted me?'

Mary experienced acute distress when the boy Jesus was missing in Jerusalem and it took her and Joseph three days to find him (Luke 2:41–50). Will you feel as stressed if you cannot find Jesus in your retreat? 'I have God's work to do', the boy Jesus said to his overwrought mother. She did not understand the full implications of those words, nor do we, at the time, understand some of the ways God treats us. Mary had Jesus to herself for those long hidden years at Nazareth (Luke 2:51–52). It was a very ordinary, humdrum, monotonous, routine existence. Perhaps your retreat will be like that. No special feelings, lights, illuminations or experiences; very ordinary and not what you hoped for. Yet the Holy Spirit is always at work in the 'ordinary' and it is in the weeks following the retreat that you will begin to realise what God has been saying to you.

I love St Mark's description of Mary going to look for Jesus (Mark 3:32), after he had left home and begun his public ministry. This again is a marvellous description of why you come into retreat . . . a time when you are looking for Jesus.

But what if your retreat turns to dust and ashes and doubts, darkness and bewilderment about God and his dealings with you try to take over? Well, that will be a bit of a privilege, like standing at the foot of the cross with Mary. There is a lovely little glimpse in Acts 1:12–14 of Mary, mothering the infant Church with her prayers. She is doing this for you in your retreat. Mary's life was so ordinary. She did nothing spectacular, she was not a preacher or teacher or organiser. Her reactions were so normal. 'How can this come about, since I am a virgin?', she asked the archangel Gabriel when she was invited to be the mother of Jesus. 'My child, why have you done this to us?', when worried and anxious she at last found him in the temple after losing him for three days.

The YES she always made to God was written deep within the silence of her heart and she only shares it with those close to her, Joseph and her cousin Elizabeth (Luke 1:39–40). She was a woman of silence and as you share her silence in your retreat, she will take you straight to Jesus, if you will let her.

Am I aware of Mary as my close travelling companion in my pilgrimage to heaven? She walks by me all the time, never getting in the way, keeping my eyes turned always toward Jesus, whispering in my ear as once she did to the waiters at the wedding reception at Cana in Galilee when the wine was running out, 'Do what he tells you' (John 2:4). What is he telling me to do in this retreat? Mary gave an unconditional 'yes' when asked to be the mother of Jesus. She took an enormous risk, a leap into the dark, not knowing where it would lead. Am I trying to make conditions in my relationship with Jesus/God? What are the risks I am frightened of or refusing to take in my Christian pilgrimage?

Try to think of the kind of conversations Jesus had with Mary especially during the thirty hidden years when they were so close to each other in Nazareth. What are my daily conversations with Mary about? Jesus loves his mother, so my relationship with him is bound to fall short unless I do the same.

Think out the full implications of the 'Hail Mary' prayer for living the Christian life.

Hail, Mary, full of grace!
The Lord is with you.
Blessed are you among women,
and blessed is the fruit of your womb, Jesus.
Holy Mary, Mother of God, pray for us sinners,
now and at the hour of our death. Amen.

THIRD MEDITATION

Finding and losing.

Our journey to God is almost like a game of hide and seek. We are on a pilgrimage, moving on all the time and our relationship with God changes as it deepens and matures in preparation for its final fulfilment in heaven. Sometimes we feel God is very near and everything is marvellous. Sometimes he seems to have disappeared and we have to go searching. The more we search the more 'clouds and thick darkness' seem to lie round about him. We have to persevere because the test of love is faithfulness, steadfastness and not 'feelings'. Sometimes we deliberately cut ourselves off from God by wandering into habits and situations which jeopardise the relationship on our side; although however much we stray, God never stops loving us. Each time we find God it is a different kind of finding and each time we think we have lost him it is a different kind of losing. Relationships can never go back to what they once were; they can only grow and develop, often with much pain and struggle.

Mary's experience of life is a marvellous example of the 'finding and losing' journey to heaven.

(1) There was a unique kind of finding when she said 'yes' to God's request to be the mother of his Son. It was not an easy decision to make. She was just as free as we are to say 'no' to God when he asks us to do

something difficult, inconvenient and more than we feel we can cope with. We are told, 'She was deeply disturbed' by Gabriel's message. Some of the questions which surged up within her were:

(i) What would Joseph say? She was betrothed to him and busy with the plans for her marriage. Would he think that she had been unfaithful to him? Would he invoke the extremity of the Law and have her stoned to death?

(ii) How could she explain it to her parents?

(iii) Could she put up with the sneers and snide remarks of the neighbours? The askance glances and the murmurings: 'Those two, Mary and Joseph, always putting on such a show of piety and devotion . . . and now look what's happened . . . there's a baby on the way and they're not married yet . . . hypocrites!'

So on the surface there was every kind of common sense reason why Mary should have said, 'I'm sorry but I cannot do it. Ask someone else.'

(2) She found a complete affirmation of her decision when she went to share the secret with her cousin Elizabeth (Luke 1:39–56). Elizabeth had a sudden revelation from God as to why Mary was coming. She cried out, 'Of all women you are the most blessed and blessed is the fruit of your womb. Why should I be honoured with a visit from the mother of my Lord?' Mary was so overcome by this that she burst into the ecstatic song of the Magnificat . . . one of those exalted moments of finding God which occur perhaps once in a lifetime.

(3) The finding of Jesus in his birth at Bethlehem was puzzling. She had never anticipated the sordid surroundings of a stable. The first visitors, the shepherds,

were not noted for being very religious. The nature of their work made it impossible to keep all the Jewish religious rules. The second visitors, the three Wise Men, were foreigners, non-Jews, Gentiles. It meant Mary was finding new aspects of God; her thinking was broadening (Luke 2:19).

(4) Did she feel God had deserted her and Joseph and the child when they had to flee for their lives and become refugees in Egypt? (Matt. 2:13–18). It was a country they disliked because the Egyptians worshipped graven images. This was totally abhorrent to the Jewish idea of God.

(5) Eventually they got back home. Then there was the anguish of losing Jesus in the Temple on their visit to Jerusalem. It was a relief to find him. The response of Jesus to being found, 'Did you not know I must be busy with my Father's affairs?', compelled Mary to reflect and find new meaning as to who her son was (Luke 2:45–50).

(6) There followed the long humdrum years of village life at Nazareth. The monotonous daily routine (Luke 2:51–52). It lasted almost thirty years. There was nothing spectacular or unusual to report. Yet it was in the ORDINARY that the relationship between the mother and the son deepened. Mary found a closeness she had never known before. It can be the same for us as we plod through the daily routine of our lives.

(7) She then had to lose him to his public life. It was not easy to 'let go'. She went looking for him (Mark 3:31–35), but there was no return to the old relationship. She could only deepen it and find him now by her prayer.

(8) At last she found him again (John 19:25–27). It was the kind of finding she had never anticipated when she made her initial 'yes' to God. She stood by the cross. She was suffused by maternal anguish. Are these the hands that once clung round her neck in childhood? Are these the feet she first taught to walk? But far worse was the spiritual torment. Why should God allow this to happen; the suffering of the innocent? For her this was the end. She did not know he would rise from the dead. It was all over. Had she made a mistake in consenting to be his mother? Her dreams were totally shattered. The sword of grief, loss, anguish and questioning was piercing her heart (Luke 2:34–35).

(9) And so she lost him to the tomb. As the stone rolled across the door of the tomb everything seemed dead, lost and without meaning. It is an authentic part of the journey to God which we all have to experience. Mary has been there before us.

(10) The resurrection of Jesus. No words can ever describe what this meant to Mary. It was a unique finding.

(11) There was a new kind of losing when her son ascended into heaven. After that she had to be content to find him in the way in which we do; through prayer, reflection and the Eucharist.

(12) At last the day came for the final finding. The voice of Jesus,

> 'Come then, my love,
> my lovely one, come.
> For see, winter is past,
> the rains are over and gone.
> The flowers appear on the earth.
> The seasons of glad songs has come . . .

Come then, my love,
my lovely one, come.'

(S. of S. 2:10–13).

So Mary was taken up into heaven. She will never be separated from her son again. 'I held him fast, nor would I let
him go.' The finding and losing of her earthly life are over.
She is busy mothering us with her prayers. We look forward
to being with her and rejoicing in the beauty of God.

Look back over your own life and reflect (like Mary) on the
times when you have found God and the times when he
seems to have disappeared. The journey is one of constant
change and growth. At times it is painful and puzzling; at
others radiant with tranquillity and discovery. We can never
go wrong if we follow Mary's advice, 'Do what God tells
you.' She did.

FOURTH MEDITATION

Mary's song on her visit to her cousin Elizabeth (Luke 1:46–55).

The Magnificat

My soul glorifies the Lord,
my spirit rejoices in God, my Saviour.
He looks on his servant in her lowliness;
henceforth all ages will call me blessed.

The Almighty works marvels for me.
Holy his name!
His mercy is from age to age,
on those who fear him.

He puts forth his arm in strength
and scatters the proud-hearted.
He casts the mighty from their thrones
and raises the lowly.

He fills the starving with good things,
Sends the rich away empty.

He protects Israel, his servant,
remembering his mercy,
the mercy promised to our fathers,
to Abraham and his sons for ever.

It is important to see Mary within the context of the history of the time in which she lived. She was a devout Jewess, believing that the Jews were specially chosen by God to reveal his true nature to the world. She and all her race hated being under the domination of the Roman empire. They were constantly looking and longing for a deliverer (a Messiah). Some thought of the Messiah in military terms, as someone who would lead a revolt against the Roman tyranny. Others thought in more religious terms of someone who would bring justice and peace and mercy for the poor and afflicted. Every married Jewish woman wondered and longed to be the one who would give birth to this Messiah.

The Magnificat is a totally Jewish song. The Messiah is to be only for the Jews: 'He protects Israel (the Jewish race), his servant, remembering his mercy, the mercy promised to our fathers, to Abraham and his sons for ever' (Luke 1:54–55). It was a shock to Mary to have to realise her child was not just to 'save' the Jews but was for everyone. The first intimation of this was at her purification, when the aged Simeon took her child into his arms and said he was to be 'a light to enlighten the pagans' (Luke 2:32). Later came the visit of the Wise Men with their gifts. They were non-Jews. So Mary had much to ponder about. It was such a contrast to the way she had been brought up to think.

The first words of the Magnificat are about praise and thanksgiving:

> 'My soul glorifies the Lord,
> my spirit rejoices in God, my Saviour.'

Thanksgiving should always have the first place in our relationship with God. There is so much we take for granted. We tend to make our prayer about our own wants and needs and the sufferings of other people, continually complaining before God.

'He looks on his servant in her lowliness;
henceforth all ages will call me blessed.'

What a prophetic statement! Some kind of intuition about her future place in the scheme of Christian redemption, her name in the middle of the Christian creed, her role as Mother of the Church, her future messages from God at the great Marian shrines of Christendom, for example, Lourdes and so many others.

'The Almighty works marvels for me.
Holy his name.'

We can take these words into our own hearts as we consider the marvels God works for us. All he does for us and gives us in baptism, confirmation, confession, unction and, above all, in the Mass and the continual presence of the risen Christ in the reserved sacrament. The beauties of nature, the warmth of the sun, our food, our drink, our friends, and our children.

All we can do is utter that great gasp of gratitude, wonder, admiration and amazement 'HOLY'.

'His mercy is from age to age,
on those who fear him.'

The mercy of God is beyond all telling. It flows endlessly through the centuries. We only have to turn to him and he opens his arms and we begin again. One of the main sources of God's mercy is seen in the sacrament of reconciliation. He gave it to us, so that time and time again we could experience his mercy. We only have to confess our failures and immediately he picks us up, welcomes us and sets out with us on a new beginning. In the story of the prodigal son, as soon as the father saw his son in the distance, 'he was moved with pity and ran to the boy'. He did not even know whether his son was returning to say sorry for having left home or coming to say he had made a great success of things. He was just glad that he had come back home. God's mercy always gets the better of him! Each time we leave the confessional God is welcoming us back home.

> 'He puts forth his arm in strength
> and scatters the proud-hearted.
> He casts the mighty from their thrones
> and raises the lowly.'

The image of Mary in popular piety tends to be that of a picture on the cover of an old-fashioned mothercraft magazine . . . caring, sweet, gentle, submissive. How does this fit in with the political, revolutionary statements of the Magnificat quoted above?

Mary had suffered under the tyranny of the Roman empire. It was because, 'Caesar Augustus issued a decree for a census of the whole world to be taken . . .' (Luke 2:1–6) that she and Joseph had had to make that uncomfortable journey to Bethlehem in the final stages of her pregnancy. Because of that she gave birth in the squalid conditions of a stable rather than in the familiar surroundings of her own home with her own mother and friends to help her. She shared the longings of her race to be set free from Roman slavery. She is a strong, determined woman; a woman committed to the liberation of the poor and marginalised from the social injustices under which they suffered. Who are the 'proud-hearted' she calls on God to scatter? Caesar and all his minions, who keep a tight hold over the Jewish people. Who are the 'mighty to be cast from their thrones'? Caesar again. Who are the 'lowly' who are to be raised? The Jewish people who, like herself, had experienced poverty, suffering, inconvenience and flight and exile in Egypt. It may have been the Jewish king Herod who was responsible for the slaughter of the innocents, necessitating Mary and Joseph to take refuge in Egypt, but Herod was a tool in the hands of Rome (Matt. 2:13–23).

Mary continues her vigorous political statements and says,

'He fills the starving with good things'.

Who are the 'starving'? They are her own people, starved of freedom and the right to run their own country, seeking their own system of justice and the freedom to worship God without being surrounded by the graven images and symbols of the Roman gods. And Mary continues,

'Sends the rich away empty.'

Who are the rich? The ostentatious Romans who have been driven out, leaving everything behind ... Such was the dream of many Jews who prayed that God would send them a saviour (a Messiah) to lead them in revolution. Mary too must have been influenced by this thinking as she pondered over the future of the child in her womb. Perhaps it was not until her Assumption that she entered into the fullness of the truth that Jesus, her son, is God from God, Light from Light, true God from true God.

All the famous valiant women of the Old Testament lead up to Mary. She is their crown. They all foreshadow the political implications of the Magnificat. Political and social justice, equal rights and the common good are the signs of mercy of the Messiah King, which his mother and hand-maiden sings. Consider:

• *Miriam* who rejoices in the liberation of her fellow Jews from their Egyptian slavery: 'Sing of Yahweh: he has covered himself in glory, horse and rider he has thrown into the sea' (Exod. 15:21).

• *Deborah*: the prophetess and judge marching with the Israelites into battle (Judg. 4 and 5).

• *Jael*, another remarkable and resourceful woman is extolled: 'Blessed be Jael among women', the war song says (Judg. 5:24).

• *Hannah*, feeling in her flesh that God had heard her plea (1 Sam. 2).

• *Judith*, who delivered Israel from the tyranny of Holofernes (the whole of the book of Judith in the Apocrypha).

IV. A Patchwork Retreat

FIRST MEDITATION

(Luke 15:11–32). Read through this familiar story. Read it again VERY SLOWLY and rhythmically (one word as you breathe in and the next word as you breathe out).

The lost son (the prodigal) and the dutiful son.

vv.11–13 He also said, 'A man had two sons. The younger said to his father, "Father, let me have the share of the estate that would come to me". So the father divided the property between them. A few days later, the younger son got together everything he had and left for a distant country where he squandered his money on a life of debauchery.

vv.14–20 'When he had spent it all, that country experienced a severe famine, and now he began to feel the pinch, so he hired himself out to one of the local inhabitants who put him on his farm to feed the pigs. And he would willingly have filled his belly with the husks the pigs were eating but no one offered him anything. Then he came to his senses and said, "How many of my father's paid servants have more food than they want, and here am I dying of hunger! I will leave this place and go to my father and say: Father, I have sinned against heaven and against you; I no longer deserve to be called your son; treat me as one of your paid servants." So he left the place and went back to his father.

vv.21–24 'While he was still a long way off, his father saw him and was moved with pity. He ran to the boy, clasped him in his arms and kissed him tenderly. Then his son said, "Father, I have sinned against heaven and against you. I no longer deserve to be called your son." But the father said to his servants, "Quick! Bring out the best robe and put it on him; put a ring on his finger and sandals on his feet. Bring the calf we have been fattening, and kill it; we are going to have a feast, a celebration, because this son of mine was dead and has come back to life; he was lost and is found." And they began to celebrate.

vv.25–30 'Now the elder son was out in the fields, and on his way back, as he drew near the house, he could hear music and dancing. Calling one of the servants he asked what it was all about. "Your brother has come" replied the servant "and your father has killed the calf we had fattened because he has got him back safe and sound." He was angry then and refused to go in, and his father came out to plead with him; but he answered his father, "Look, all these years I have slaved for you and never once disobeyed your orders, yet you never offered me so much as a kid for me to celebrate with my friends. But, for this son of yours, when he comes back after swallowing up your property – he and his women – you kill the calf we had been fattening."

vv.31–32 'The father said, "My son, you are with me always and all I have is yours. But it was only right we should celebrate and rejoice, because your brother here was dead and has come to life; he was lost and is found."'

Reflection

Write down which of the characters in the story you identify
with most. Say why.

vv.14–20 The prodigal son comes to terms with his own
situation: he faces reality; he realises the blame is his. What
are the situations in my own life that I refuse to face? At
home? At work? In the church where I worship? Within
myself? Write them down. How far do I make excuses and
blame other people?

v.20 There were no conditions to the father receiving him
back. The father when he saw the son a long way off, did
not know whether the son was coming to tell him of success
or failure. He made no conditions. Do I make conditions
about relationships? Or before I will forgive others? Do I
accept others as they are or am I trying to change them into
what I think they ought to be?

vv.22–24 The very things which had led to his downfall
through debauchery are the things which are used to
welcome him home – fine clothes, jewels, wine, good food,
music and dancing. What does this tell me about the good
things of this life?

vv.25–32 It is so easy to resent newcomers in situations
where I have a long established and respected position. It
can happen in the congregation where I worship, in the place
where I earn my living or in the clubs and organisations
where I take my recreation. Do I feel threatened? Do I
refuse to accept and co-operate with the new situation? Do
I make disparaging remarks about the newcomer and am I
unhelpful and unwelcoming?

The father in the story represents God. The elder brother thinks his father loves the erring brother more than him. Do I think God is like this? Am I really pleased and delighted that God's love falls equally on the just and the unjust? To whom do I think I am superior? Why? Would God agree? Write a prayer which expresses your own relationship to God. Does it bear the marks of a love letter?

Sit still for 15 minutes DOING NOTHING.

SECOND MEDITATION

Holiness.

Read each of the following three times, slowly and reflectively:

'Yes, it is I, Yahweh, who brought you out of Egypt to be your God: you therefore must be holy because I am holy' (Lev. 11:45).

'Before the world was made, he chose us, chose us in Christ, to be holy and spotless . . .' (Eph. 1:4).

'Be holy in all you do, since it is the Holy One who has called you, and scripture says: *be holy, for I am holy*' (1 Pet. 1:15–16).

It is in our daily lives and not exclusively in our religious exercises that we climb the road to heaven. Our religious exercises (prayer, Eucharist, penance, etc) are pauses for essential refreshment en route.

What kind of image floats into your mind at the mention of the word 'holiness' or 'perfection'? Is it religious professionals like priests, monks or nuns? Why not a truck driver, a solicitor, an actress or the person at the checkout in the supermarket? Is 'holiness' a complicated business involving special training? Or is it very simple?

Surely, if God is closer to us than we are to ourselves, if

he created us with a great desire that we should be 'holy',
then 'holiness' should be the normal condition of mankind.
It is what we are meant to be; not by any special esoteric
means, but by our daily job or even unemployment; and for
most, by marriage and the bringing up of a family. This is
exhilarating. From every single event in our daily lives,
however trivial, we learn something about ourselves. All
growth in self-knowledge is the work of the Holy Spirit and
therefore a new glimpse of God, of 'holiness'. So then, no
experience is wasted. We can't lose out! Everything is grace.
'The heavenly Jerusalem is not in some dream in the future.
It is now. One only needs to open one's eyes'
(Abhishiktananda).

Why then, if it is so simple, won't we accept it? We don't
want to learn. We prefer other goals. Comfort, a variety of
ambitions, success and, of course, money, particularly
winning the lottery. We want life to be smooth. Every jolt,
pain, stress and affliction becomes an interruption, something to get round. In fact they are the footholds of reality –
of 'holiness'. It is not very easy to think of 'holiness' as
NOW, when something has gone badly wrong or we have
lost someone or something we desperately need, or we
have made a mistake. The panic and stew we get ourselves
into tells us a great deal about our own condition. Every
event, however trivial, every moment is a revelation and so
often a painful one. If we pay attention to our reactions to
the various demands made upon us we can tell which parts
of ourselves are shaky, rotten and self-centred. In contrast
we are given a glimpse of our true selves, our true CENTRE,
'the place in a man where God bears witness to himself'.
We must listen to ourselves.

When I congratulate someone on his or her success, is
there deep within me a bell of envy ringing? When I com-

miserate with someone on their disappointment or misfortune, is there hidden within me a secret note of pleasure and satisfaction? Yes, we muffle it up. Even to ourselves. But it is the first note which speaks the truth. Each one of us has, with the help of the Holy Spirit, to work on ourselves. The reluctance we had to go out of our way to do an errand for someone or visit the sick and housebound. The cowardice when we did not get up and refute a speaker because it would make us unpopular. The time we give if we have to prepare to talk to important people but do not give if it is only to old age pensioners.

We must practise, day by day, bearing the pain of self-discovery. It is not the least depressing, even when the rotten parts of ourselves are disclosed. Then we can let the Holy Spirit work on us. Good habits can be acquired, just as bad ones can. So much can be done by treating the ordinary events of every day as spiritual exercises. Is this depressing? NO. Once we get our breath back, after the first shock of discovering these truths about ourselves, we begin to enjoy living in the truth rather than in a cloud of illusion about ourselves. We discover the particular diseased areas of ourselves which need healing.

Healing is a slow process. We begin to perceive that it is happening when our outlook on the world and people changes from being negative and destructive into one of light and joy.

All areas of experience, however ordinary or trivial, can be areas of spiritual growth. The awful thing is that we throw them away. How easily, in today's world, people throw away a marriage or abort a baby in the womb. We try to get rid of what we don't like or want. When it is gone there is nothing left to reflect on. There is no possibility left for transformation or for the unwanted to be worked into the

wanted. Some people try to throw away their own background, especially if they feel it won't be acceptable as
they climb the ladder of 'class'. Yet we cannot destroy our
background. It has made us what we are.

In order to learn from the day it is a good thing in the
evening to switch off the TV, and sit down quietly and
reflectively, to ponder all that has happened during the day
and why and consider our reactions to all the various
people and situations of the day, or its loneliness and mono-
tony. Why did I behave as I did?

An ordered day is essential to holiness. This is not easy –
when people are still drugged with sleep at dawn, when they
switch on their TVs and radios the minute they get up and
start drinking coffee; when the lights are on, the traffic is
roaring and the TV and radio or the taped music continues
to boom away through the day and night, then the sacred
thread linking human beings to the order of creation (the
rising and setting of the sun, the waxing and waning of the
moon, the subtle changes in the seasons) gets more and
more frayed until it snaps altogether. You can get order by
following the fourteenth-century mystic Eckhart's advice:
'Holiness consists in doing the next thing you have to do,
doing it with your whole heart and finding delight in doing
it.'

A whole area, largely unexplored by most, is our dreams.
God sends crucial messages to the dreamer in the deep
silence of the night to guide us along the way of 'holiness'.
Think of Samuel (1 Sam. 3:1–18) and St Joseph (Matt.
1:18–25; 2:13, 19–23).

We have to reflect on our relationship with our neighbour,
both personal and global. We have to ask ourselves, 'Is the
job I do, my daily routine, compatible with deepening my
own relationship with God and my neighbour?' We are all

shaped by what we do for a living. What shape am I? If my work is helping to bolster up an unjust, oppressive society, what must I do about it to retain my integrity?

An ordered day is essential to 'holiness'. We are all addicted to pushing more into the day than is possible. The 'need' for instant travel, information and food is meant to give us more time and more space. It does the opposite! However, there are times when we can become addicted to order. We can't hear the voice of God breaking through the tightly ordered day we had planned. So, occasionally, we have to be prepared to 'let go'. Sometimes letting go of a small thing can change the whole of our lives. Look back into your own life and see if this is true.

What image floats into your mind at the mention of 'holiness'? Write down the names of those you know or hear about whom you class as 'holy'. Do you want to be holy? Is there anything which militates against holiness in your close relationships, your daily work, your life within the Church or your recreation, sports and hobbies?

All areas of experience (from washing up to climbing Mount Everest) can be areas of spiritual growth. What are the main areas of my daily life? How do I find God in them?

Sit still for 15 minutes and DO NOTHING.

THIRD MEDITATION

Living with doubts (John 20:24–29).

Read through the familiar account of the doubting Thomas. Read it slowly and reflectively.

v.24 Thomas, called the Twin, who was one of the Twelve, was not with them when Jesus came.

v.25 When the disciples said, 'We have seen the Lord', he answered, 'Unless I see the holes that the nails made in his hands and can put my finger into the holes they made, and unless I can put my hand into his side, I refuse to believe'.

v.26 Eight days later the disciples were in the house again and Thomas was with them. The doors were closed, but Jesus came in and stood among them. 'Peace be with you' he said.

v.27 Then he spoke to Thomas, 'Put your finger here; look, here are my hands. Give me your hand; put it into my side. Doubt no longer but believe.'

v.28 Thomas replied, 'My Lord and my God!'

v.29 Jesus said to him: 'You believe because you can see me. Happy are those who have not seen and yet believe.'

When you pray do you bring your whole self to God, or only the parts you hope he will approve of? Do you keep your doubts hidden from him? Yet the doubts are there.

How can I believe God loves and cares, when the TV

screen brings to me, almost daily, pictures of the most appalling sufferings being inflicted on people who have done nothing to deserve it? What about genocide? Or as you watch the coffin slide into the crematorium furnace, do you wonder, is that person still alive in eternity?

If we are really to pray, instead of playing a polite game with God, then we must be totally open with him. We must stop treating God as a touchy stranger from whom we hide our true feelings and doubts. We must let our doubts out into the open and see if he has any way of dealing with them, instead of thinking he is cross about them!

The Psalms make no bones about it. They form a wonderful prayer book and one used by Our Lord himself. They are very ancient, but they still live because they express every conceivable human emotion, in every kind of situation. Love, joy, fear, depression, gratitude, tranquillity, grief, revenge, doubt, hatred and anger. They are all there. What better expression of doubt than 'O my God, I cry in the daytime and thou hearest NOT.' So then, where is he? Perhaps he is not there at all!

Of course, our doubts don't surge unto full force until we meet personal and unexpected tragedies, have to face an incurable illness, or begin to wonder what is the point and purpose of our lives. Nevertheless there are some doubts which are lurking about all the time and a retreat is a time for looking at them.

We may be surprised to find our doubts can be allies and friends in our journey to heaven, not blasphemous enemies. Sometimes doubts can be like angels, agents of the Spirit of truth, trying to strip us of immature and superstitious beliefs. For example, doubting whether Christ is really God may be the only way in which the Spirit of God can get us to start again from scratch and believe in his total humanity.

For many committed Christians, Christ is a kind of half God who cannot possibly be a total human being. For such people the 'Word made flesh' is not a real man at heart, but God just dressed up in a male skin! He is in fact perfect God and perfect Man. So we say in the Creed:

> We believe in one Lord, Jesus Christ,
>   the only Son of God,
> eternally begotten of the Father,
> God from God, Light from Light,
> true God from true God,
> begotten, not made,
> of one being with the Father.
> Through him all things are made.
> For us men and for our salvation he came down from
>   heaven:
> by the power of the Holy Spirit
>   he became incarnate from the Virgin Mary, and was
>   made Man.

This is a mystery beyond all telling. Nevertheless as we draw closer to Our Lord, through prayer and sacrament, we become aware of its truth. We cannot explain it in scientific terms. We know it at heart. We stand on the witness and faith of countless millions of Christians who have gone before us. They shout a triumphant 'YES' to our prayer, 'Lord, I believe. Increase my faith.'

Doubts about doctrines and moral rules may be the only way the Spirit of truth can get us to move from accepting Christianity at second hand to appropriating it for ourselves in the light of our own experience and questions. The Spirit can work better in us, even if our faith is stripped right down for a time – a veritable whirlpool of doubts and un-certainties – rather than if we are coerced in a complacent religiosity which we are not prepared to have disturbed! Living in tension between the traditional teaching of the Church and contemporary opinions on all kinds of issues is not always easy. It is the tension of the cross. Trying to discover what is of God and what is of a destructive devil in our secular, materialistic society produces tension. We long for certainty and we are faced with doubt. We must pour out all our doubts, all our questions and all the dark side of ourselves at the feet of God. We must not try to hide them or repress them. God can take it!

Perhaps our worst doubt is not about some particular doctrine or ethical teaching, but something more totally overwhelming, something which has dogged the steps of would-be believers throughout the centuries. How can we believe in a totally loving God? So much seems to deny it. 'How can we sing the Lord's song in a strange land?' The strange land of the holocaust, the exploding AIDS epidemic, the scenes of violence, starvation and stress on the TV screen, the long, blood-soaked history of the churches and the awful things Christians do to one another and say about each other. How can God be love? We often try to repress this voice of doubt. We don't think we ought to have it. God won't like it. In fact, doubt is a profoundly religious experience. It takes us to the very foot of the cross, into the very heart of Jesus himself when he cried out from the cross, 'My God, my God, why have you forsaken me?' God seemed to have disappeared and the whole of Jesus' belief and past life surged up within him as a great 'doubt'.

For many struggling to believe it is not true that there is OBVIOUSLY a God. It is not true that God is obviously a LOVING God. It is not obviously true that the crucifixion of a Galilean carpenter is the AXIS on which all human destinies turn.

The experience of these doubts, far from removing us from God, should lead us into a deeper reflection on his hidden-ness and silence. 'Verily you are a God who hides yourself.'

We have to try and see what the world and life look like from the point of view of the agnostic and unbeliever. If we don't, then it is impossible to present the Christian faith to them with any 'meaning'. So it is urgent to let the Holy Spirit look at the doubts within ourselves. In this way we can be with the unbelievers where they are and live with the questions they ask – questions to which they do not see the answers in what we preach.

Doubts

Write a list of all your doubts (if any!) about Christianity and the Church. Search the book of Psalms for verses which express your doubting mood.

In what ways do you find yourself at variance with the traditional teaching of the Church on any issue? What are your reasons? Can you find any biblical authority for them?

We live in a state of tension between asserting 'God is love' and then trying to square it with the terrible things people (including Christians!) do to each other. Do you think of this tension as a profoundly religious experience which can plunge you into the heart of Jesus? God is not always obvious. What was going on in the mind of Jesus when he took on his lips the words of Psalm 22 as he hung dying on the cross?

Try and work out what the world and life looks like from the point of view of the unbeliever. If we cannot do this how can we present the Christian faith to them with any meaning? So it may be an urgent matter to let the Holy Spirit make us attend to the doubts within ourselves.

Sit still for 15 minutes DOING NOTHING.

FOURTH MEDITATION

Affirmation.

'Well done, good and faithful servant; you have shown you can be faithful in small things, I will trust you with greater; come and join in your master's happiness' (Matt. 25:21).

Listen to Our Lord. Can you hear him saying, 'Thank you for all the things you do for me'? God thanking us? How do you feel about it? Is it a totally new idea? Write down a list of all the things Our Lord is thanking you for. Yes, he is grateful to you. Perhaps it makes you feel tearful or you are nonplussed because the whole idea seems unthinkable. It is intriguing. It opens up a whole new area in your relationship with Our Lord. Can you come to terms with it?

Do you only think of Christ in terms of the relentless demands he seems to make on you? Do you feel you are only a servant doing your duty in a master/slave relationship? Thanks don't enter into it. Listen. Our Lord is saying, 'Thank you for all the things that you do for my body, the Church; thank you for all you do for your neighbours, for the poor, for your friends and for your family. Thank you for letting me come into your heart in Holy Communion. I was waiting for you.' Is this a wonderful new slant on your relationship with Jesus? It makes the right balance to the continual beating of your breast and crying out 'Kyrie eleison.'

Perhaps you have a poor self-image? It clouds that right

self-love, that right self-affirmation, which Jesus says is an absolute necessity before we can love our neighbour in the right way. 'You must love your neighbour as yourself' (Matt. 19:19; 22:39).

If you feel uncomfortable at the thought of Jesus saying 'thank you' to you, ask yourself the question, 'What do you think of people who never say "thank you" to you?' Would you like to think of Jesus in the same way.

We each have our gifts. 'The Spirit apportions to each one individually as he wills' (1 Cor. 12:4–11). ' . . . the same Spirit who distributes different gifts to different people just as he chooses'. It is important that we should know what they are and affirm and realise that the right use of them gives great joy to God because they are reflections of himself. He is so full of happiness when we use them. Alas, so many people won't affirm their talents. That is mock humility. Instead of using your own gifts, are you always wishing you had somebody else's? That is childish. You can find out if you appreciate your own gifts by asking yourself:

1) Am I good at recognising, affirming and thanking God for the gifts of others and speaking of them to others with gratitude? Or am I jealous and envious and do I show it by making snide, untrue and critical remarks?

2) Am I delighted when someone else is a great success?

The truth is that you will never be able to affirm in others what you put down in yourself. Only when we recognise the delight Christ has in the things we do well for him, through grace, will we be able to participate with him in delighting in the different gifts of our fellow men and women.

Perhaps you are diffident about your own gifts? When you do something well, you only think of how much better you could have done it or make falsely modest, deprecating remarks about it, and saying 'it's nothing really'. Conventional, traditional piety, which is the way many people have been brought up, says that we are always in such danger of pride, that we must continually be dowsing our hearts with the cold waters of self-depreciation in order to keep us humble!

We are so corroded with self-doubt. Even when we boast, we are really compensating for a deep inner lack of belief in our own gifts. We imagine that we are being humble, but true humility comes from the affirmation of our gifts, the recognition that they come from God. They are not accidents and God has such delight in our use of them that he can say, 'Well done, good and faithful servant' (Matt. 25:21).

True humility is our sense of our need for each other; for completeness: that my gifts complement yours and yours supplement mine. True humility arises from the vision of our interdependence within the web of life.

Our Lord invites us, 'Come and join in your Master's happiness' (Matt. 25:21). We not only share his happiness when he is saying 'Well done' to us but also his great joy in dwelling in our midst in the blessed sacrament. 'My delight is to dwell among the sons of men', he says, and 'I am risen and am still with you.' He loves being in our midst; he is faithful to his words, 'this is my body; this is my blood'. He loves coming into our hearts in the act of Holy Communion.

He is also overjoyed to be able to say to us, through the lips of his priest, 'I forgive you all your sins', when we kneel in the confessional. He throws his arms around us and says, 'Welcome back home.' When we are in love we enjoy giving presents to the one we love. Let us be the same with Jesus.

For the Lord delights in you (Isa. 62:4). Consider the enormous pleasure, delight and joy it gives to God to dwell in our hearts. He won't let himself be driven out no matter how hard we pretend he is not there! He is so happy to dwell in our midst in the blessed sacrament. He loves it as he says to us 'I am risen and am still with you'. He looks forward to sharing our life intimately as he unites himself with us yet again in the act of Holy Communion. It is just as if he was giving us a big hug!

He really enjoyed being able to do so much for us at our baptism. (Write down on paper exactly what you think he did on that once-for-all occasion.) He sings 'alleluia' with us each year as we celebrate our baptism birthday.

He is delighted to welcome us back each time we make our confession. It really makes his day! Pope John XXIII said, 'I always blow Jesus a kiss in return when I have made my confession and hear him speaking through the lips of his priest saying, "I forgive you".' 'Let him kiss me with the kisses of his mouth' (S. of S. 1:2).

Jesus enjoys dwelling in everyone. 'My delighting to be with the sons of men' (Prov. 8:31). Reflect on Jesus living in the hearts of those you love and like, those you don't like or understand, those who threaten you or have hurt you, those who suffer. Sometimes we find a living Jesus, sometimes a forgotten, dying, despised and mocked Jesus. He is always there and he always loves us, however we treat him. Ponder over St John's Gospel (14:23).

Sit still for 15 minutes DOING NOTHING.